THE PROPER ECONOMIC DEVELOPMENT OF AFRICA AND ITS GLOBAL STRATEGIC IMPLICATIONS

THOMAS P. FULLER
PAUL GLUMAZ

TABLE OF CONTENTS

INTRODUCTION

The purpose of this report is to discuss the economic ideas of Lyndon LaRouche as these could be applied to the rapid development of Africa. In so doing, this report will also discuss the problems of finally freeing Africa from a brutal economic colonialism that has yet to end, which also means freeing Africa from the mercenary proxy warfare used by the West to prevent African development. Further, this report will also discuss the sovereign financial means that could be established that could finance the major infrastructure projects that would be essential to any African economic development. Included in this will also be an outline of the projects that would be needed.

Further, this report comes at a time where the system of speculative finance that rules Africa, and the world, and its incredible monumental debt structures is now coming into its final collapse, especially in the context of the serious global pandemic of the coronavirus and its effects on the global supply-chain. This report will discuss measures African nations can take for economic sovereignty in the opportunity represented by the collapse of the financial system at the center of Africa's financial colonial masters.

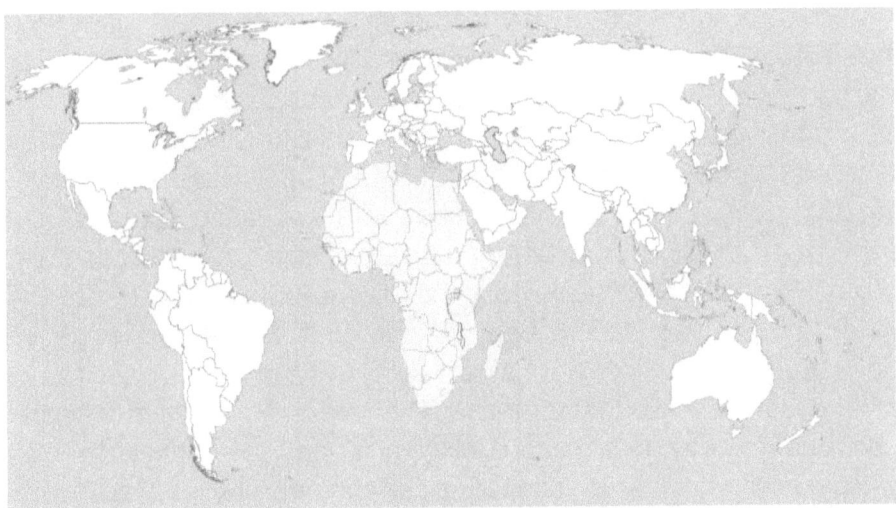

Why Lyndon LaRouche?

Lyndon LaRouche's economic ideas hold the key to the conceptual map that African leaders need for their economic strategies of development. Neo-liberal economics will not work for the development of Africa. Marxist economics will also not work for the development of Africa. What will work is the physical economic science of Lyndon LaRouche. This science is echoed in the earlier economic development of the United States, Germany, and Japan, the means and methods of which have not been taught in Western universities for at least a century. Larouche's science of physical economics is not ideological. Right versus Left, Capitalism versus Socialism, free market versus dictatorship, and other such dichotomies are all based on false ideas about economics that are taught in Universities in the West and are promoted to confuse and corrupt African leaders.

What are LaRouche's credentials?

First, Lyndon LaRouche is the most vilified and slandered intellectual, economist, and political figure in the West. This vilification has occurred because LaRouche's philosophical and economic ideas are seen as a grave threat to the continuing "colonial" oppression of most of the world, especially Africa. Second, every effort has been made in the West to suppress the truth that China's current Belt and Road initiative, which potentially promises to lay the groundwork for the full industrialization of the world. To a significant degree, the Belt and Road Initiative originates as an extension of Lyndon LaRouche's economics in what was presented to China in the early 1990's as the World Landbridge. In this regard, Helga Zepp LaRouche, Lyndon LaRouche's wife, is known in China as "the new silk road lady."

PHYSICAL GEOGRAPHY AND THE NEO-MALTHUSIAN TERROR OF DEMOGRAPHICS

The bare statistics of Africa's arable land potential and population characteristics are astounding. The narrative that surrounds these figures is even more astounding in its contradictions.

On the one hand we are told that mankind and Africa have surpassed their agricultural bio-sustainability. On the other hand, we are told that Africa has anywhere from 200 to 600 million hectares of arable land not under cultivation – with varying figures of 50% to 60% of the world's arable land not under cultivation. Again, on the one hand we are told the population explosion in Africa will lead to more food insecurity, poverty, and famine, while on the other hand, we are told that Africa could be the food basket for the world.

The entire landmass of Africa is 30.3 million square kilometers. This is roughly three times the land area of the U.S. or China. The current estimate of Africa's population is 1.34 billion. But the most amazing statistic is that the median age of all Africans is 19.7 years and the population growth rate is somewhere around 2.6%! Compared to other areas: The median age in Europe is 42.6 years, in the U.S. is 38.2 years, in China it is 38.4 years, and in Japan it is

47.3 years. Africa's median age in youth even dwarfs that of India at 26.8 years. The Hoover Institute projects a population for Africa at 2.5 billion by 2050. Other estimates are higher. That close to 60% of the increase in world population by the year 2050 will come from Africa!

MEDIAN AGE COMPARISON

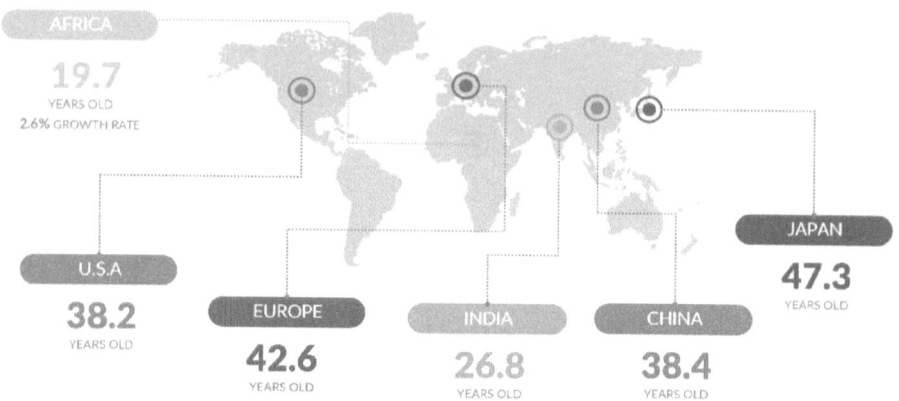

To some, this is great news because population is a good thing. To others, this projected population growth in Africa is the greatest threat to the existing power structure and identity of those who still harbor a racist colonial mentality towards Africa, whether disguised or not. The issue is development. Can Africa develop such that its current and future population can be far more effectively productive? If so, humanity has a good chance of survival. If not, humanity will probably not survive.

World Population Forecast with Africa's percentage share

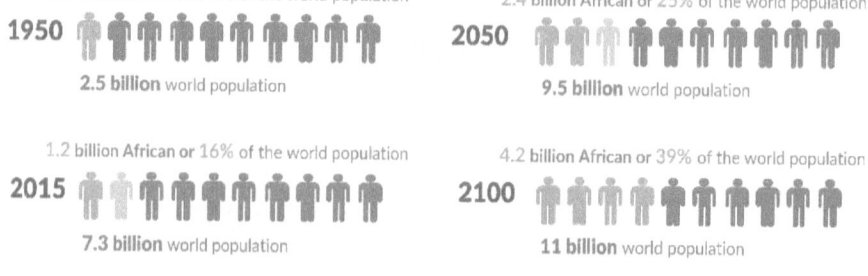

230 million African or 9% of the world population
1950
2.5 billion world population

2.4 billion African or 25% of the world population
2050
9.5 billion world population

1.2 billion African or 16% of the world population
2015
7.3 billion world population

4.2 billion African or 39% of the world population
2100
11 billion world population

Source: UNICEF

Around 1800 the British East India Company sponsored the now famous, or infamous Thomas Malthus, who promoted the concept that population increases at a greater rate than the capacity to support the population. Later his population thesis was credited by Charles Darwin as being the inspiration for Darwin's development of the concept of Natural Selection, which in turn became the basis for the concept of the "survival of the fittest" doctrine that justified the genocide of the then ruling British Empire, as well as race science, and later Hitler's justification for exterminating whole populations.

Coat of arms of the East India Company circa 1700's. Photo by: **TRAJAN 117**

This viewpoint was revised and extensively promoted in the early 1970's as "limits to growth." That the "population bomb" was the greatest threat to mankind. Along with this came the changes in culture within the more affluent and developed nations. Since then the birth rate in these nations has dropped to almost zero, in some cases below zero. Today, most developed nations are only increasing their populations through immigration from the less developed areas of the world. In these more developed nations instead of a population growth crisis, there is a crisis of the lack of population growth.

Fortunately for humanity, the inhabitants of Africa have a demonstrable disagreement with the overpopulation narrative. Unfortunately, however, the racism of the old colonial mentality is still in force with a vengeance for reducing world population, if not through economic means, then perhaps through famine, plagues, and even perhaps through nuclear war.

In 1974, a secret study was done under Henry Kissinger that was called NSSM 200, or National Security Study Memorandum 200. NSSM 200 claimed that the population growth in areas such as Africa was a greater strategic national security threat to the U.S. than the Soviet Union. This report was only declassified in the early 1990's. This orientation has yet to be officially repudiated by the U.S. government.

Twenty years later, in 1994, there was a United Nations population conference in Cairo, Egypt, that attempted to set up sanctions for nations, especially African nations, whose populations were increasing. Fortunately, there was a hue and cry around the world and eventually Bill Clinton had to back down on having the U.S. force through the U.N. a population's growth sanctions regime.

More recently these efforts to curtail, if not reduce Africa's population, comes under the code words, "sustainability," and "ecology." "Sustainability" means development without industrialization. "Ecology" means Africa must be denied access to the carbon-based energy resources needed to develop because of the "climate emergency." The fraud of this is obvious because the same promoters of "sustainability" and "ecology" also wish to prevent Africa from having nuclear power which has no carbon "footprint." To be frank, "ecology" and "sustainability" are more modern labels for the same old racist genocide of the past.

THE BASIC LAWS OF PHYSICAL ECONOMY

Lyndon LaRouche has written an entire corpus of material on the science of physical economy, including the textbook, So You Wish to Learn About Economics. What follows is a discussion of some of the ideas of Lyndon LaRouche on the science of physical economics to give a sense to the reader that there are lawful principles governing the development of an economy that are universally applicable for all societies, regardless of their level of development, or system of government. The reader is encouraged to go beyond this to explore in more depth the writings of Lyndon LaRouche.

PRODUCTIVE VERSUS OVERHEAD

To begin with, LaRouche looks at the economy as a single physical entity encompassing the entirety of production and consumption as part of the ongoing physical reproduction of a society. Within that totality there are important distinctions in terms of the activity of individuals who are producing and consuming what is produced. The first distinction is that of the family, which is the unit of reproduction, and is the primary unit in any description of the economy. Second, these family units are divided between those who are involved in the actual process of production, whether manufacturing, mining, agriculture, construction, or transportation and those who are not. Those who are not are what is called "overhead." This could be the service sector, administration, military, education, entertainment, and most of all the financial sector.

The fact that this distinction is not made in the accounting of Gross Domestic Product, GDP, leads to a distortion of the actual productive reality in economic statistics. This is because the economic activity "overhead" is combined and not distinguished from actual production. In this respect, GDP figures can be seriously delusional in terms of the actual health of a nation. In other words, the activities of those who consume the actual product, but do not produce the product, should not be counted in the GDP. It is only recently that China has begun, under China's Premier, Le Keqiang, to do away with GDP figures, and instead of GDP figures, use actual production figures as a measure of the economic product of an economy.

All that is produced beyond the means of sustaining the families of those who are producing is called surplus. That which is produced beyond sustaining the families of productive operatives as well as the rest of the society called overhead, is called "net surplus." How much "net surplus" there is and how it is deployed determines the future growth of an economy, and if there is none, there is a future lack of development, or a decline of the total economic reproductive system.

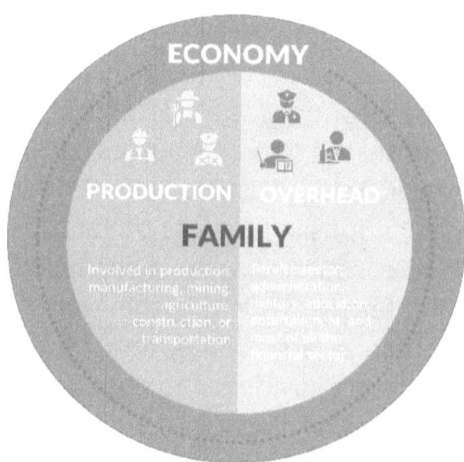

If the overhead becomes too large relative to the productive capacity through such things as usury, or the unsustainable consumption of the non-productive part of society, a society must decline, or in many cases, offset the tendency to decline by military expansion, which in turn increases the overhead and the need to expand further through the procurement of what is not being produced from some other society. This is the physical economic definition of all empires, including colonial empires. On the other hand, productive societies that produce "net surplus" will tend to want to trade that net surplus with other productive societies to obtain goods that will further help to develop that society and their economy. Today, many of the Asian societies, especially China would fall into this category.

RELATIVE POTENTIAL POPULATION DENSITY

The measure of any society's economy is by the potential population that can be sustained by that economy. From this comes LaRouche's term "relative potential population density." A society whose relative potential population density is increasing at an increasing rate is a society that is developing. A society, which instead is not increasing its relative potential population density at an increasing rate, is a society that is not developing.

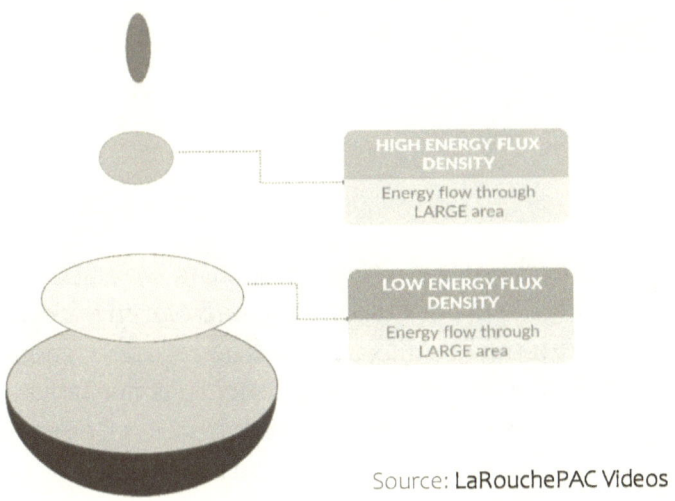

HIGH ENERGY FLUX DENSITY
Energy flow through LARGE area

LOW ENERGY FLUX DENSITY
Energy flow through LARGE area

Source: LaRouchePAC Videos

ENERGY FLUX DENSITY

All societies run into a problem of limited resources in any given fixed level of technology and culture. The existing culture, knowledge and technology define a resource availability. As the easier to obtain resources are used up, the population and productive activity of the economy must expand to get at the harder to get resources. This problem of having to expand for less will ultimately lead to a collapse of the society. To escape the limited resource problem all societies must find ways to redefine the resource parameter through scientific and technological progress. The most important variable for this qualitative and quantitative increase in available resources is something LaRouche calls "the increase of the energy flux density" of the energy used to refine raw materials and produce goods.

WILLFULL HUMAN ANTI-ENTROPY

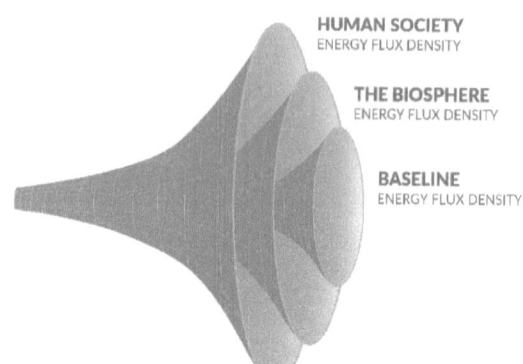

HUMAN SOCIETY
ENERGY FLUX DENSITY

THE BIOSPHERE
ENERGY FLUX DENSITY

BASELINE
ENERGY FLUX DENSITY

FUEL	WEIGHT EQUIVALENT
WOOD	23.5 TONS
COAL	6.15 TONS
OIL	30 BARRELS
FISSION	1.86 GRAMS
FUSION	0.57 GRAMS
ANTIMATTER	0.22 GRAMS

Source: LaRouchePAC Videos

Whenever there is an increase as from wood burning to coal, or coal to petroleum products, or from petroleum products to nuclear fission, or from nuclear fission to nuclear fusion, there is a greater than exponential increase in what becomes available as a resource which before was not a resource. Energy Flux Density is defined by the intensity of energy flowing through a cubic centimeter at the point of use. That increase, the increase of energy flux density, is what defines the available resources, not any fixed limit. It is for this reason that CO_2 was chosen as the environmental villain, because all higher energy density applications beyond wind, and solar, involve fossil fuels. Outlawing a and curbing fossil fuel use is intended to prevent any further economic development, and cause as well a physical economic collapse of society. This is the current wishful intention for Africa of the colonial powers in deploying the Green movement.

14

ECONOMIC PLATFORM

Economic platforms are defined by the mode of energy production and use, the cultural level of the population, level of technology, the internal composition of capital, and the amount of population. These economic platforms are only possible within maximum and minimum boundaries.

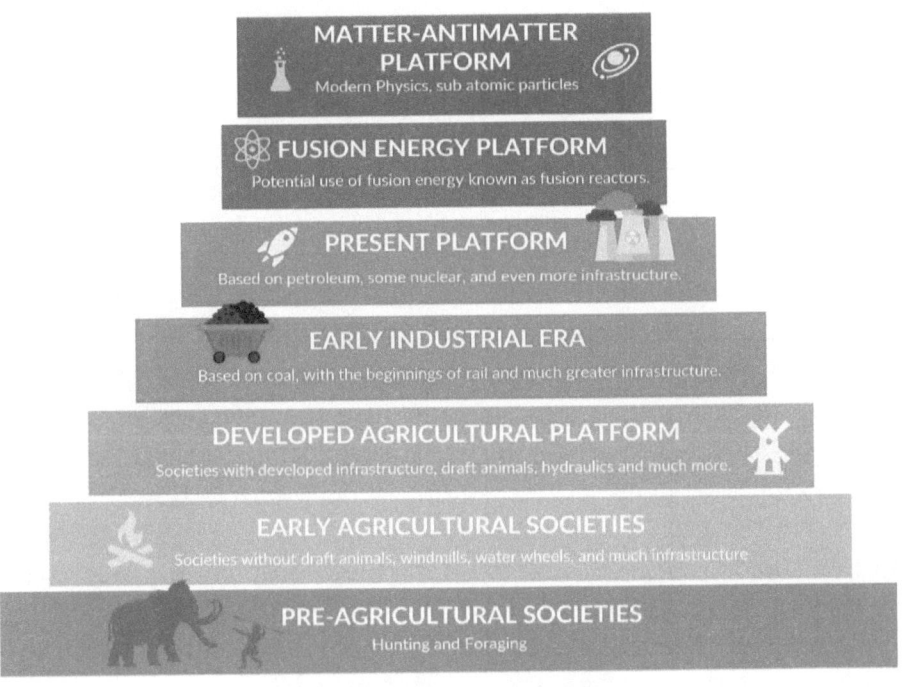

ECONOMIC PLATFORMS

At the lowest level you have pre-agricultural societies. At the next platform you have early agricultural societies without draft animals, windmills, water wheels, and much infrastructure. Next you have much more developed agricultural platforms with much more developed infrastructure, draft animals, perhaps hydraulic works, and more. The next platform is the early industrial era primarily based on coal, with the beginnings of rail and much greater infrastructure. Next you have the platform of today based on petroleum, some nuclear, and even more infrastructure. Last there is the potential fusion energy-based platform that will dramatically alter the productive potential of humanity by several orders of magnitude beyond what we have today.

Each of these platforms has a minimum population and complexity of the division of labor required to keep society in that platform, and a maximum population that that platform can sustain. Moving from one platform to another creates exponential increases in terms of relative potential population density. The key parameter to this is the concept of "energy flux density."

DIVISION OF LABOR AND THE COMPOSITION OF CAPITAL

In all societies there is a division of labor in the production of what is consumed to sustain a society. To go from one platform to another the division of labor of that platform must be vastly expanded and with that a dramatic increase in the population within an economy. For instance, the idea that automation will create the need for less people because machines will ultimately replace human labor at the point of production is a gross misunderstanding common today in economic thinking. The opposite is the case. Such a move to automation requires a much greater division of labor and a much greater population. For every worker replaced at the point of production, many more workers would have to be employed to service, design, program, train, educate, and maintain the increased soft as well as hard infrastructure needed to sustain an increase in automation.

Within the division of labor of an economic platform there is a distinction between what is called "variable capital" and "constant capital." Variable capital is all the production consumed by the all the family units of the workforce. Constant capital is what is consumed in the creation and maintenance of the tools and machinery used in the production and the associated "hard" infrastructure. As one goes progressively from one platform to another, from a lower potential population density to a higher one, there must be a shift toward an increase of constant capital relative to variable capital. Transportation infrastructure must increase in amount and efficiency of travel and communication. More factories are needed, etc. Relatively more and more production must be consumed by the infrastructure component of the economy in order to increase the productive power of the economy. This is especially important for any African nation.

CONSTANT CAPITAL

All the production consumed by the building and maintaining of infrastructure plant, and equipment.

Fixed assets, i.e. plant, machinery, land and buildings

VARIABLE CAPITAL

All the production consumed by the families of all those involved in the production of all goods.

Refers to the cost of maintaining productive labor

Factories can be set up to employ relatively inexpensive labor, but without an infrastructure transformation, there will only be marginal development, and living standards will not improve. This is often referred to as the "middle income trap," but is much worse than some kind of "trap" for the world. This is because the application of the exploitation of low wage labor in infrastructure deficit areas of the world leads, in physical economic terms, to the lowering of the relative potential population density of the world economy. This is because the more infrastructurally developed part of the world economy ends up with a decreasing productive capability and an increasing overhead in the consumption of the products of the less developed countries, while the less developed countries infrastructure is not developed. This leads to both a lack of increase in the ratio of Constant Capital to Variable Capital globally, and an increase of Overhead relative to ability to support that overhead, ultimately causing a decline of the relative potential population density, or the productive power of the total world economy taken as a whole.

On the other hand, if the more developed part of the world were to increase its already developed infrastructure to assist in exporting capital goods to develop the less developed world, then wages would rise globally, as the less developed parts of the world undergo transformation to a higher infrastructure based productive platform.

In this case, the potential relative population density of the planet would dramatically increase along with a global rise in living standards. All versions of neo-Liberal economics, the Keynesian ones, as well as the more Classical Conservative ones, are absolute curses to humanity. Their application, since especially the post-1971 takedown of the Bretton Woods system, has dramatically lowered the global relative potential population density of the planet. In contrast to this, China's effort in the Belt and Road Initiative is today the only major policy that is contrary to this curse.

LAROUCHE'S FOUR LAWS

LAROUCHE'S FOUR LAWS:

The next, most extensive section of this report deals with the application of LaRouche's economic ideas to the development of

Africa. This will be done by first introducing LaRouche's written application of his economic ideas in his document *The Four New Laws to Save the U.S.A. Now! Not an Option: An Immediate Necessity.*

Although written specifically for the U.S., this document by LaRouche, written in 2014, has in it the basic action plan that all nations need to adopt to deal with the current systemic financial and physical collapse of the world's economy. This report will take each Law presented in LaRouche's report, and develop around each Law, the underlying principles conceptually, historically, and currently as they apply to the development of Africa.

The Four New Laws to Save the U.S.A. Now! Not an Option: An Immediate Necessity
By Lyndon H. LaRouche, Jr.

The Fact of the Matter

The economy of the United States of America, and also that of the trans-Atlantic political-economic regions of the planet, are now under the immediate, mortal danger of a general, physical-economic, chain reaction breakdown-crisis of that region of this planet as a whole. The name for that direct breakdown-crisis throughout those indicated regions of the planet, is the presently ongoing introduction of a general "Bail-in" action under several or more governments of that region: the effect on those regions, will be comparable to the physical-economic collapse of the post-

"World War I" general collapse of the economy of the German Weimar Republic: but, this time, hitting, first, the entirety of the nation-state economies of the trans-Atlantic region, rather than some defeated economies within Europe. A chain-reaction collapse, to this effect, is already accelerating with an effect on the money-systems of the nations of that region. The present acceleration of a "Bail-in" policy throughout the trans-Atlantic region, as underway now, means mass-death suddenly hitting the populations of all nations within that trans-Atlantic region: whether directly, or by "overflow."

The effects of this already prepared action by the monetarist interests of that so-designated region, unless stopped virtually now, will produce, in effect, an accelerating rate of genocide throughout that indicated portion of the planet immediately, but, also, with catastrophic "side effects" of comparable significance in the Eurasian regions.

The Available Remedies

The only location for the immediately necessary action which could prevent such an immediate genocide throughout the trans-Atlantic sector of the planet, requires the U.S. Government's now immediate decision to institute **four specific, cardinal measures: measures which must**

Greenbacks were paper currency issued by the United States during the American Civil War.

be fully consistent with the specific intent of the original U.S. Federal Constitution, *as had been specified by U.S. Treasury Secretary Alexander Hamilton while he remained in office: (1) immediate re-enactment of the Glass-Steagall law instituted by U.S. President Franklin D. Roosevelt, without modification, as to principle of action. (2) A return to a system of top-down, and thoroughly defined, National Banking.*

The actually tested, successful model to be authorized is that which had been instituted, under the direction of the policies of national banking which had been actually, successfully installed under President Abraham Lincoln's superseding authority of a currency created by the Presidency of the United States (e.g. "Greenbacks"), as conducted *as a national banking-and-credit-system placed under the supervision of the Office of the Treasury Secretary of the United States.*

For the present circumstances, all other banking and currency policies, are to be superseded, or, simply, discontinued, as follows. Banks qualifying for operations under this provision, shall be assessed for their proven competence to operate as under the national authority for creating and composing the elements of this essential practice, which had been assigned, as by tradition, to the original office of Secretary of the U.S. Treasury under Alexander Hamilton. This means that the individual states of the United States are under national standards of practice, and, not any among the separate states of our nation.

(3) *The purpose of the use of a Federal Credit-system, is to generate high-productivity trends in improvements of employment, with the accompanying intention, to increase the physical-economic productivity, and the standard of living of the persons and households of the United States.* The creation of credit for the now urgently needed increase of the relative quality and quantity of productive employment, must be assured, this time, once more, as was done successfully under President Franklin D. Roosevelt, or by like standards of Federal practice used to create a general economic recovery of the nation, per capita, and for rate of net effects in productivity, and by reliance on the essential human principle, which distinguishes the human personality from the systemic characteristics of the lower forms of life: the net rate of increase of the energy-flux density of effective practice. This means intrinsically, a thoroughly scientific, rather than a merely mathematical one, and by the related increase of the effective energy-flux density per capita, and for the human population when

considered as a whole. The ceaseless increase of the physical-productivity of employment, accompanied by its benefits for the general welfare, are a principle of Federal law which must be a paramount standard of achievement of the nation and the individual.

(4) *"Adopt a Fusion-Driver 'Crash Program.'" The essential distinction of man from all lower forms of life, hence, in practice, is that it presents the means for the perfection of the specifically affirmative aims and needs of human individual and social life.* Therefore: the subject of man in the process of creation, as an affirmative identification of an affirmative statement of an absolute state of nature, is a permitted form of expression. Principles of nature are either only affirmation, or they could not be affirmatively stated among civilized human minds.

Funeral of US President Warren G. Harding. Horse drawn coffin in procession outside of the White House.

Given the circumstances of the United States, in particular, since the assassinations of President John F. Kennedy, and his brother, Robert, the rapid increase required for even any recovery of the U.S. economy, since that time, requires nothing less than measures taken and executed by President Franklin D. Roosevelt during his actual term in office.

The victims of the evil brought upon the United States and its population since the strange death of President Harding, under Presidents Calvin Coolidge and Herbert Hoover (like the terrible effects of the Bush-Cheney and Barack Obama administrations, presently) require remedies comparable to those of President Franklin Roosevelt while he were in office.

This means emergency relief measures, including sensible temporary recovery measures, required to stem the tide of death left by the Coolidge-Hoover regimes: measures required to preserve the dignity of what were otherwise the unemployed, while building up the most powerful economic and warfare capabilities assembled under the President Franklin Roosevelt Presidency for as long as he remained alive in office. This meant the mustering of the power of nuclear power, then, and means thermonuclear fusion now. Without that intent and its accomplishment, the population of the United States in particular, faces, now, immediately, the most monstrous disaster in its history to date. In principle, without a Presidency suited to remove and dump the worst effects felt presently, those created presently by the Bush-Cheney and Obama Presidencies, the United States were soon -finished, beginning with the mass-death of the U.S. population under the Obama Administration's recent and now accelerated policies of practice.

There are certain policies which are most notably required, on that account, now, as follows:

Vernadsky on Man & Creation

V.I. Vernadsky's systemic principle of human nature, is a universal principle, which is uniquely specific to the crucial factor of the existence of the human species. For example: "time" and "space" do not actually exist as a set of metrical principles of the Solar system; their admissible employment for purposes of communication is essentially a nominal presumption. Since competent science for today can be expressed only in terms of the unique characteristic of the human species' role within the known aspects of the universe, the human principle is the only true principle known to us for practice: the notions of space and time are merely useful imageries.

Rather:

The essential characteristic of the human species, is its distinction from all other species of living processes: that, as a matter of principle, which is rooted scientifically, for all competent modern science, on the foundations of the principles set forth by Filippo Brunelleschi (the discoverer of the ontological minimum), Nicholas of Cusa (the discovery of the ontological maximum), and the positive discovery by mankind, by Johannes Kepler, of a principle coincident with the perfected Classical human singing scale adopted by Kepler, and the elementary measure of the Solar System within the still larger universe of the Galaxy, and higher orders in the universe.

Or, similarly, later, the modern physical-scientific standard implicit in the argument of Bernhard Riemann, the actual minimum (echoing the principle of Brunelleschi), of Max Planck, the actual maximum of the present maximum, that of Albert Einstein; and, the relatively latest, consequent implications of the definition of human life by Vladimir

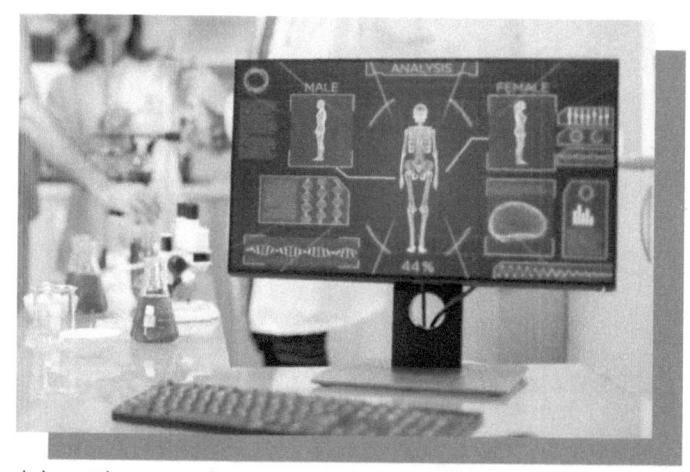

Ivanovich Vernadsky. These values are, each relative absolutes of measurement of man's role within the knowledge of the universe.

This set of facts pertains to the inherent fraud of the merely mathematicians and the modernist "musical performers" since the standard of the relevant paragon for music, Johannes Brahms (prior to the degenerates, such as the merely mathematicians, such as David Hilbert and the true model for every modern Satan, such as Bertrand Russell, or Tony Blair).

The knowable measure, in principle, of the difference between man and all among the lower forms of life, is found in what has been usefully regarded as the naturally upward evolution of the human species, in contrast to all other known categories of living species. The standard of measurement of these compared relationships, is that mankind is enabled to evolve upward, and that categorically, by those voluntarily noëtic powers of the human individual will.

Except when mankind appears in a morally and physically degenerate state of behavior, such as within the cultures of the tyrants Zeus, the Roman Empire, and the British empire, presently: all actually sane cultures of mankind, have appeared, this far, in a certain fact of evolutionary progress from the quality of an inferior, to a superior species. This, when considered in terms of efficient effects, corresponds, within the domain of a living human practice of chemistry, to a form of systemic advances, even now leaps, in the chemical energy- ux density of society's increase of the effective energy- flux-density of scientific and comparable expressions of leaps in progress of the species itself: in short, a universal physical principle of human progress.

The healthy human culture, such as that of Christianity, if they warrant this affirmation of such a devotion, for example, represents a society which is increasing the powers of its productive abilities for progress, to an ever-higher level of per-capita existence. The contrary cases, the so-called "zero-growth" scourges, such as the current British empire are, systemically, a true model consistent with the tyrannies of a Zeus, or, a Roman Empire, or a British (better said) "brutish" empire, such as the types, for us in the United States, of the Bush-Cheney and Obama administrations, whose characteristic has been, concordant with that of such frankly Satanic models as that of Rome and the British empire presently, a shrinking human population of the planet, a population being degraded presently in respect to its intellectual and physical productivity, as under those U.S. Presidencies, most recently.

Chemistry: The Yardstick of History

We call it "chemistry." Mankind's progress, as measured rather simply as a species, is expressed typically in the rising power of the principle of human life, over the abilities of animal life generally, and relatively absolute superiority over the powers of non-living processes to achieve within mankind's willful intervention to that intended effect. Progress exists so only under a continuing, progressive increase of the productive and related powers of the human species. That progress defines the absolute distinction of the human species from all others presently known to us. A government of people based on a policy of "zero-population growth and per capita standard of human life" is a moral, and practical abomination.

Man is mankind's only true measure of the history of our Solar system, and what reposes within it. That is the same thing, as the most honored meaning and endless achievement of the human species, now within nearby Solar space, heading upward to mastery over the Sun and its Solar system, the one discovered (uniquely, as a matter of fact), by Johannes Kepler. A Fusion economy, is the presently urgent next step, and standard, for man's gains of power within the Solar system, and, later, beyond.

LAROUCHE'S FOUR LAWS

DISCUSSION OF THE FIRST LAW

FIRST LAW, BANKING SEPARATION:

The first law applied internationally is banking separation, or a firewall between the internal commercial financial activity within a nation, and any financial activity that involves investments of any kind such as stocks, bonds, currencies, commodities, venture capital, speculation and other types of investments. This firewall existed in the U.S. between 1933 and 1999 and was named Glass-Steagall after the two legislators who originally introduced the measure into the U.S. Congress: U.S. Senator Carter Glass and U.S. Representative Henry B. Steagall.

Carter Glass and Henry B. Steagall sponsored the Glass–Steagall Act of 1932 separating commercial and investment banking.

The importance for Africa is that no development is possible internally in an African nation without a protected commercial banking sector. Without a protected commercial banking sector there will be a lack of ability and flexibility to expand lending for commercial activity. Without the ability for individuals and businesses to safely and soundly deposit their savings and operational funds at local financial institutions which are regulated by this firewall, economic activity is restricted to a much lower multiplier to the amount of currency in circulation for lack of savings on which to base commercial lending, as there is no means from preventing any financial institution from using the deposits for non-commercial purposes and speculation. Further, without this banking separation, there will be a lack of ability to maintain secure and stable local financial institutions. This then leads to a situation where local savings will either go offshore, outside the nation, or will be maintained by hoarding either the local currency, or most likely a foreign currency like the U.S. dollar, or the Euro. In this case a dependency is created on a foreign currency which can only be obtained at the expense of the ability to have a sound and secure local commercial banking system.

On the other hand, if a protected depository commercial banking system exists, local financial institutions can turn deposits of currencies into loans at a ten to one ratio, thus giving one unit of currency deposited a ten unit of currency economic power. This is because when a bank makes a loan, it creates money in circulation, when a loan is paid back, money is taken out of circulation. If the commercial banking system is not protected in this way, deposits will be used for purposes other than commercial activity, causing a diminution of the funds available locally for economic activity. This is the big problem we have today in the developed nations' repeal of these protections that used to exist.

Alexander Hamilton, the first Treasury Secretary of the United States, is the actual creator of the original commercial banking sector. Hamilton develops this in his first report to the U.S. Congress on credit. At the founding of the U.S., the U.S. was bankrupt because it could not pay the massive debt contracted in the revolutionary war. How many African nations have been in a situation where the debts cannot be paid, and the IMF and the creditors are demanding "structural adjustments" just like the original situation at the founding of the U.S?

What Hamilton did as first Treasury Secretary was a miracle that all African nations could do. Instead of defaulting on the war debt, or further destroying the nation by taxing the nation to obtain the gold and silver to pay the debt, Hamilton reorganized the debt into income bearing Treasury notes. These Treasury notes were in small enough denominations and could be obtained by individual citizens by turning worthless war debt called Continentals, with a portion of gold and silver, and in return receive a secure income from doing so. Holding Treasuries was better than hoarding gold or silver as savings, making Treasuries instead, a preferred form of savings. As a result, all the debt of the revolutionary war, a debt that could not be paid, was converted into productive and useful capital. Prior to this, the fluctuations in the value of the Continentals made only gold and silver of value. This allowed the hoarded gold and silver not in circulation to instead be deposited in local banks, also earning a small return, from which the local banks could then issue bank notes as currency. This meant that instead of gold and silver being hoarded as savings, the gold and silver in circulation could be expanded as credit by the bank notes ten times. This increased credit for commercial activity rapidly expanded the economy of the otherwise bankrupt nation which had just come into existence.

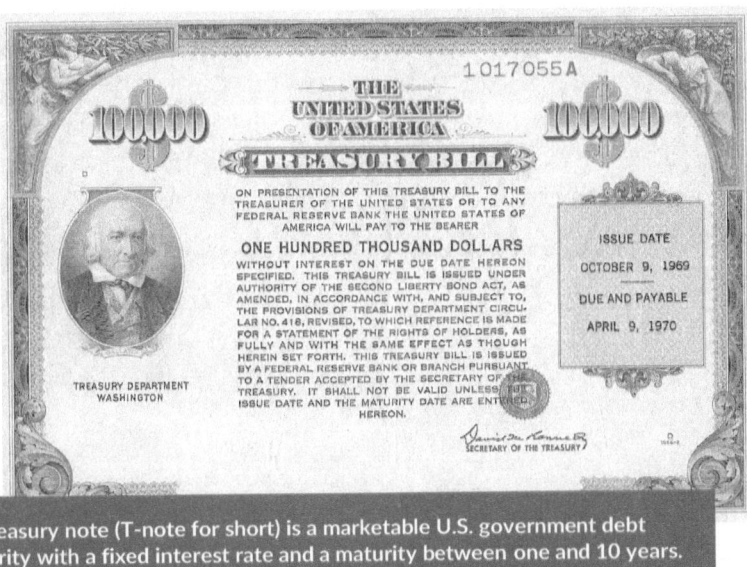

A Treasury note (T-note for short) is a marketable U.S. government debt security with a fixed interest rate and a maturity between one and 10 years.

By this, a new system had emerged on earth that empowered a nation and its people to have the means to engage in economic activity with such credit and power for vast undertakings. There is no precedent in history for this. This is the real American revolution in economics that was called the "American System." This was the invention of Alexander Hamilton whose ideas have been erased for over a century from the memory of modern liberal economic academic study. What today's bankers of the City of London, and Wall Street fear the most, is the revival of an understanding of Alexander Hamilton, especially in Africa. If African intellectuals begin studying Hamilton's reports to the U.S. Congress, they will be amazed at the intellectual deception and the criminality involved in the obscuring of the works of Alexander Hamilton. Such intellectuals may also begin to better understand how they have been deceived by their Western education.

In the more modern developed nations, it had been previously customary for governments to insure the deposits in the commercial banks up to a certain point. That is because when local banks are not trusted, it is hard to have a functioning commercial banking system. However, once that protection was removed by repealing laws like Glass-Steagall, governments ended up bailing out the speculation-oriented investment banks which had merged with the commercial banks, to avoid facing a collapse of the whole system, a collapse, which because rampant speculations will eventually happen regardless.

Thus, the first law of Lyndon LaRouche is the installment of Glass-Steagall, or bank separation laws that create a protected commercial banking sector.

LAROUCHE'S FOUR LAWS

DISCUSSION OF THE SECOND LAW

SECOND LAW PART I: NATIONAL BANK, OR A CREDIT SYSTEM NOT A MONETARY SYSTEM

The second law of LaRouche is that all nations in order to develop must establish a National Bank, or equivalent, in order to have a sovereign credit system. To develop a nation means big projects or undertakings which only an institution such as a National Bank could provide the financing for. The credit emitted by a National Bank is credit that is sovereign. What sovereign credit means is that the credit in circulation is owed to the nation and its citizens as a whole, for which the National Bank and the credit system serves. The nation creates credit which it lends to itself and circulates the credit for the purpose of engaging the productive powers of its population.

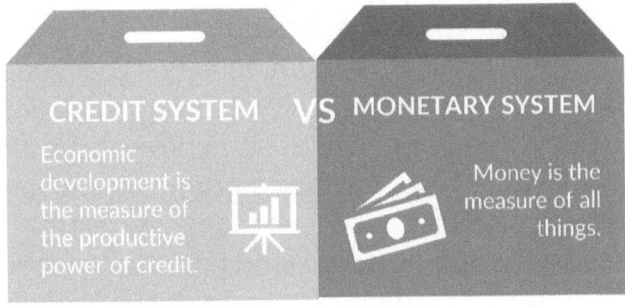

In a sovereign national credit system, the availability of credit is based on what needs to be done and the value of the credit is based in what it does. In a sovereign national credit system, the credit that is circulating as currency, or money, is not the measure of wealth, or value. Rather, sovereign credit is the means to engage the society in the process of creating wealth that gives value to the credit. In a sovereign credit system, credit is created by, and is a power assigned to government whose sole responsibility is to the general welfare.

In contrast, a monetary system, as opposed to a credit system, is a system of slavery to the Money in circulation that is created by independent central banks whose function is NOT TO DEVELOP A NATION, but rather to manipulate the supply of money and interest on that money. The supply of money in circulation by central banks is primarily tied to the purchase of government debt. The interest and principal on the debt of governments that is bought and sold is backed by the taxing power of government. The major purchasers of government debt, that sell this debt to the central bank for a commission, are the major private financial institutions. These financial institutions then multiply as loans the funds received from the central banks for the sale to the central bank of government debt. This lending by the private banking sector of monetized government debt is what becomes the increase of money in circulation. The crux of the matter is that private bankers, who monetize this government debt through loan deposit multipliers, have no obligation to use this monetized debt for any kind of local or national development, or general welfare. Yet governments and the population pay the private banking sector for access to this monetized government debt!

In a monetary system, money is the measure of all things. In a monetary system, to carry out any endeavor requires access to money, but if one cannot somehow obtain the money, or provide assets as security for that money, the endeavor cannot be carried out. In a credit system, economic development is the measure of the productive power of credit. To carry out an endeavor in a credit system, all one must show is that the endeavor has value for the community and the nation, and credit will be available. The activity generated by that endeavor is the security for the credit.

Does any African nation today have a sovereign credit system? Or, are African nations merely the slaves of monetary systems controlled by their former colonial masters? Wherever money is the measure of value, and not the means to create value, a people is enslaved to money.

This is part of the Second Law of Lyndon LaRouche. This is also what Alexander Hamilton created in the early American republic. This is what is discussed at length in Hamilton's second report to the U.S. Congress, On National Banking.

SECOND LAW PART II: THE COLLAPSE OF THE INTERNATIONAL CITY OF LONDON FINANCIAL SYSTEM

Monetary systems must ultimately collapse through unsustainable debt that is not backed by physical production, or the inability to obtain further plunder not backed by physical production to cover the debt.   What follows is some essential history on the nature of monetary systems.

The rapacious European colonial expansion and its continuing plunder through a monetary system till today, has its origins in a Venetian banking system that controlled the trade in the Mediterranean and the trade in gold and silver currency exchanges between Europe and the East. The European Renaissance in the 1400's threatened the power of Venice, and Venice launched religious wars in response, drowning Europe in blood. This is similar to the jihadi and mercenary wars of today promoted by the modern continuators of the Venetian tradition.

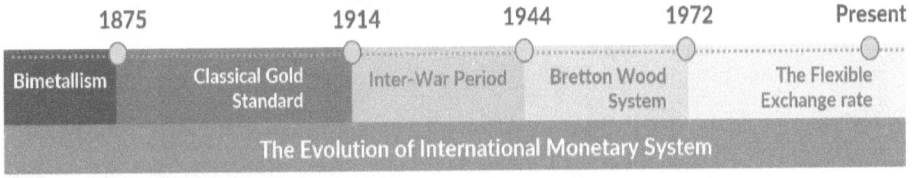

In the second half of the 1600's, Venice moved its operations first to Amsterdam, and ultimately to London in the late 1600's and early 1700's. Unfortunately, the great advances in science and technology of the European Renaissance, which should have been used for the good, became the basis of the more advanced military power used by the Europeans to subjugate the planet, under Venetian type monetary systems. The main global resistance to this in the late 1700's was the English-speaking colonies in North America and Russia.   That is why to this day, the principal geopolitical objective of the current neo-colonial system has been to keep Russia, in whatever form, and the successor to the English-speaking colonies in America, in constant conflict. The potential cooperation of these two powers has been the greatest potential threat to the current continuation of the Venetian system in the City of London and its secret offshore financial jurisdictions.

The current, modern form of the Venetian monetary system of empire begins with the ascendancy of the British East India Company. At the Treaty of Paris in 1763, ending the Seven Years War, the British East India Company – a private company with a royal charter founded in 1600 – emerged with the power to plunder and loot India and thereby became the most powerful imperial entity in the world. Since then, the British East India Company and its successors have continued to be the greatest imperial power on the planet. Through this emergence of the power of the British East India Company, and through its takeover of India, the British East India Company was able to begin imposing the same looting policies on the English-speaking colonies. The resistance – resistance to this looting carried out in collaboration between the British East India Company and the British Monarchy – is what led to the American Revolution. The continuation of the British East India Company in its modern form, along with its international auxiliaries, is the power that has unabatedly continued into the present, looting Africa and most of the world.

From 1763 to the present the principal enemy of this empire, has been the United States and its Industrial potential coming out of the U.S. Civil War, and World War II, and its alliances in those periods with the other principal enemy of this empire, Russia. Subversion and attempts to recruit and/or destroy the U.S. and Russia, whether through wars, promotion of cultural decadence, and/or corruption of their elites has been the determining historical process since the founding of the U.S.

During WWII, U.S. President Franklin Roosevelt told Churchill of his intention to end the colonial looting system and bring to the world the policies of industrialization, especially to the newly soon to be independent nations. The way Roosevelt intended to do this was to end the gold monetary system of the British pound sterling, the center of their monetary empire, and replace that system with a system of sovereign credit governed by sovereign nations. This became the fixed exchange system agreed to at Bretton Woods Conference in 1944. However, the original intentions of the Bretton

Woods system envisioned by FDR were compromised. Instead Truman was induced by the British to start the cold war with the Soviets, something FDR had not intended. It is thereby that the original institutions of the World Bank and the IMF were subverted during the Cold War and did not fulfil their original intention of helping to finance the development of the nations that were becoming nomically independent, as FDR had also intended. The cold war allowed for the unfortunate return of this system of empire, initially through undermining of the original Bretton Woods System under the guise of fighting Communism, and later with the Vietnam war and the creation of an offshore dollar system which ultimately led to the ending of the Bretton Woods system.

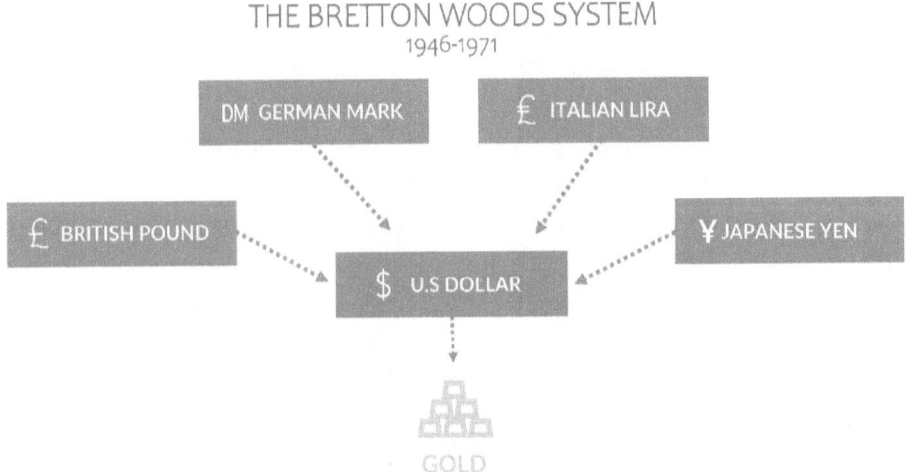

THE BRETTON WOODS SYSTEM
1946-1971

By 1971 to 1973 the same colonialist forces were successful in overthrowing the Bretton Woods fixed exchange system and replacing it with a system based on currency speculation. They did this through a process of creating an offshore secrecy jurisdiction outside the law, and outside the U.S. and all national jurisdictions which allowed investments to obtain higher returns than was legal in nations under the Bretton Woods system. This included most of all the proceeds from the illegal drug trade and other criminal activity. This was done in complete violation of the international laws governing capital controls that were part of the Bretton Woods system. These secrecy jurisdictions all connect to the one square mile special jurisdiction known as the City of London. Eventually over the subsequent 47 years the ability to further develop any nation, whether in Africa or the more developed nations has become increasingly impossible. This system is now finished and is collapsing.

The collapse of this system will impact Africa hard, but it also represents opportunities for Africa to use the collapse to leave the monetary system and go into a credit system. Instead of a dark age and mass depopulation, what could emerge from this collapse could be the following.

First, a new international financial architecture must be established similar in some respects to the former Bretton Woods fixed exchange system. Every nations currency will be pegged at a fix rate to all other currencies. Each nation will have something like a Hamiltonian National Bank that will internally provide credit for internal development. The currency of each nation will be sovereign in that nation, and will not be speculated on. Exchange of currencies will be for trade. Clearing houses in each nation will carry out these exchanges. To facilitate adjustments in the fixed rate between nations, gold will be used as a reference. These adjustments are by sovereign agreement between nations and not by the marketplace and the speculators. This will facilitate the vast expansion of exports to the less developed world of capital goods for infrastructure and industrialization. These exports which will complement China's Belt and Road, will economically invigorate the decaying developed nations and lead ultimately to an end of poverty in the world by 2050.

SECOND LAW PART III: THE HISTORICAL LACK OF SOVEREIGN CREDIT IN AFRICA

The historical lack of sovereign credit among African nations has severely blocked and frustrated Africa's economic developmental intentions. Whether in the colonial period, where the credit was controlled by the colonial power, or in the neo-colonial period where credit is controlled by international finance, so aptly described by Kwame Nkrumah in his book, *Neo-Colonialism, the Last Stage of Imperialism*, the resolution of this problem is central to any future African development. It should be noted that there has not yet been a post-colonial period for Africa. The term post-colonial is a fraudulent deception. Historically there is the pre-colonial period, the colonial period, and the neo-colonial period. There is no post-colonial period. That period is yet to come. It can and it should. Nominal political sovereignty is not sovereignty. Economic sovereignty is real sovereignty. Once that exists, then the science of physical economic as developed by Lyndon LaRouche, and historically based in the earlier Hamiltonian development of the U.S., Japan, Germany, and currently China can be applied to fully industrialize Africa.

19th-century print of slavers bringing captives on board a slave ship on Africa's west coast.

The two types of monetary systems that existed in Colonial Africa were the French African Franc administered by the Bank of West Africa established in 1901 as an expanded continuation of the 1853 Banque du Senegal, and the British monetary version, the colonial currency board. Both operated somewhat differently but had the intention of replacing, as much as possible, the use force to extract labor and raw materials, with the use of money.

For the European colonies in Africa, whether of a settler variety, or of an administrative variety, the primary purpose of having a colony was to produce and extract products for the international market at the cheapest cost. These products would be of two primary categories, plantation products, and raw materials. Any economic infrastructure, such as ports, roads, and rail would only be constructed for administrative, and extractive purposes. In this respect nothing fundamentally has changed in this regard since the post 1971 resurgence of the same system after the failure of the Bretton Woods system. Today's international "rules-based order" of the IMF, GATT, WTO, etc., is the same in principle for the world as the earlier colonial system of Africa.

The primary issue for the European colonies was how to obtain the "cheap" labor slavery for the mines and plantations when Africans would rather prefer to exist in their agricultural self-subsistence communities. One method that was used prior to the U.S. Civil war was the slave trade. The slave trade was an old system used by the Romans, the Ottomans, the British, the Dutch, the Spaniards, etc. However, a slave trade requires a market for slaves. The victory of the Union army in the U.S. and the rapid industrial transformation of the U.S. during and thereafter, ended much of that market. Better means had to be found. It is only in this context that one can understand the evolution of monetary systems in the African colonies.

In the French colonial zone, the 1901 created Bank of West Africa (BWA) was instrumental in this. In the founding of the BWA there was a merger of the BWA with the major privately held African French trading houses based in Marseilles and Bordeaux. The growth of currency emission and use in French Africa was tied to the growth of extraction for the international market. Prior to this, despite forced labor laws, it had been much more difficult for the French to get the cheap labor needed.

However, creating a demand for the French Franc was not easy. One way to do this was to make the African French Franc the only way to pay head taxes, and other taxes levied by France. Thus, Francs were necessary and became available from the Bank of West Africa in exchange for labor. Another way was to indebt the indigenous leadership and get them to participate in encouraging those under them to leave their community and work the plantations and the mines. The circulation of the French Africa Franc was deliberately restricted to prevent other uses than the looting required for the international market. Transitioning their African

Sénégal. - DAKAR. - La Banque de l'A. O. F.

Bank of West Africa (BAO) 1904

subjects to the use of money, rather than local barter systems of exchange, was the major challenge for the French in exploiting the labor of the colonies without the costly use of simply rounding up workers by force, as had been done earlier.

A similar problem occurred in India with the British who could not induce labor to leave their local caste areas. The lack of extensive control in the rural areas was a big factor in the 1857 Sepoy Mutiny in India that almost overthrew the British East India Company rule. As a result, the British crown took over from the British East India Company and carried out some "reforms." The greatest of these reforms was "famine relief," otherwise explained as "charity." To get labor to leave the local areas, the British deliberately induced famines on a rotating basis. Those dying in the villages were given the choice of leaving the village to work in famine relief camps. Those who did not, died. Those who did, lost

Distribution of famine relief in the Madras Presidency. From the Illustrated London News (May 26,1877)

their caste privileges and were forced to slave in exchange for the meager relief given and could not return to their villages or go anywhere else. The labor so exploited was essential in building much of the infrastructure of British rule. As that infrastructure grew, more remote villages became accessible to more induced famines. Along with all of this came the introduction of money. This has always been the proper definition of the British concept of "charity." To the very proper British, you must give thanks to your oppressor for the privilege of being starved to death.

The Bank of West Africa eventually morphed into the CFA Franc currency system established in 1945 at the end of WWII. The current monetary system in use in Francophone Africa is a continuation in form and practice as what existed earlier. The two central banks that oversee the two CFA Franc systems are under co-supervision of France. These central banks function to manipulate the supply of money as previously discussed and cannot invest directly in the development of any of the countries involved. And if they could, they would have to maintain 50% of the currency issued in reserve at the Banque du France. The CFA Franc is pegged to the Euro at a fixed rate. The Euro itself is a monetary unit used by all members of the European Union (EU) under a European Central Bank in which no European nation has any control. As a result, Europe has no current way to develop, and has not been developing since the European Union came into being. That is because no European nation has any control over its currency. Thus, Europe has economically declined, enslaved to a monetary system of international finance that loots all of Europe's population. In the current situation, the French nations of Africa are stuck with a CFA Franc none them controls, tied to a Euro which no European nation controls. So even if France had intentions of developing its former colonies, which it does not, it could not do so, because it cannot, under the European Maastricht agreement, even finance the development of France. Thus, the looting of Europe extends directly into French Africa.

The British version of using money to extract the wealth of their colonies involved the use of what are called currency boards. The British began using this method in 1849 in Mauritius and by the 1940's there were currency boards in 70 countries, many not directly under British rule. Using a currency board ensures there will be no development at all for the nation that uses it. A currency board, as opposed to a central bank system, cannot hold government debt as an asset on which to increase the circulation of money. The circulation of money in the colonies and in the nations that used the British Pound currency board system is completely fixed to the amount of British Pounds that are held in reserve by the currency board for the banking institution that issues the local currency. If the local private sector wishes to purchase Pounds in exchange for the local currency, the amount of local currency in circulation decreases. If the local private sector wishes to buy local currency with pounds, the amount local currency in circulation increases. There is no ability to expand currency in circulation without obtaining British Pounds whose circulation is restricted and controlled.

The advantage of a currency board for the British empire is that it unifies commercially the empire globally without the need for continuous military action. The area under the currency board is starved for credit and has no sovereignty. The private sector rules based on "supply and demand, buy cheap sell dear" where the means of exchange, currency, is dear, and everything else produced in the area under the currency board is cheap. The shortage of currency in the area makes the local currency tied to the British pound dearer than life itself, without which nothing can be done. This is like the French example and the current CFA Franc whose circulation is likewise restricted and unable to be expanded for increased economic development and activity

In the current period, since the end of the Bretton Woods system in 1971, the same forces that have run the British empire, and the currency board system, and who now run the offshore secrecy jurisdiction of the City of London, have sought to transform a national U.S. dollar into a global reserve currency they now control offshore of the U.S. outside a national jurisdiction. Using the oil crisis of the 1970's in forcing the 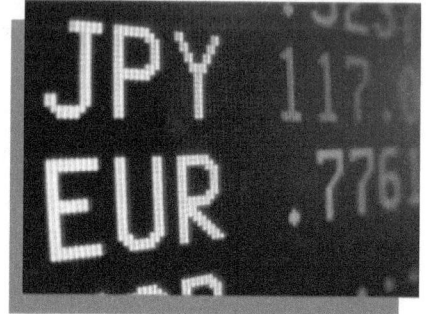 demand for the dollars required to purchase Middle Eastern oil, and using the interest rate increase of 1979 to 1982 by Federal Reserve Chairman Paul Volcker, which created massive capital flight from all over the world into U.S. Treasuries, the U.S. dollar was transformed into the replacement reserve currency of the world, with an added very nasty component of daily fluctuations of the value of the dollar on international currency markets. With the creation of the Euro, another similar reserve currency was created.

Today there is something like $5 trillion in currency speculation on the U.S. dollar daily with only a few percent of those transactions related to the actual movement of goods. Upon the projected collapse of the U.S. dollar-based system, which has been happening since September 2019, these same neo-colonial forces plan to make either gold directly, or a cryptocurrency, the new world's reserve currency controlled by the same continuing neo-colonial financial institutions. While this will not be allowed without a struggle by Russia, China, and India, as well as other countries, the lack of a new global financial architecture, like the previous Bretton Woods system, will lead to wars, chaos, famines, and depopulation.

SECOND LAW PART IV: THE FOLLY OF THE CURRENT ATTEMPTS AT A MONETARY UNION OF ECOWAS

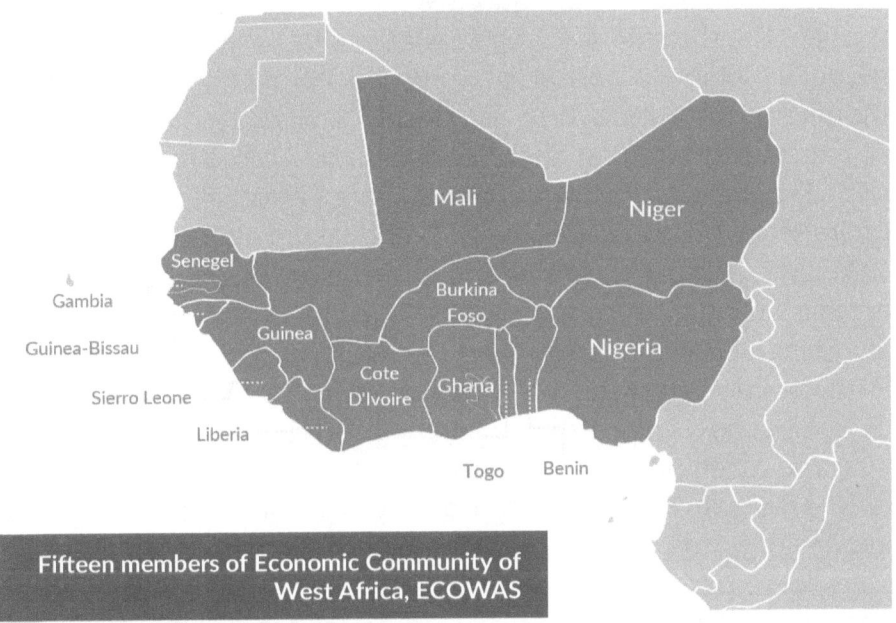

Fifteen members of Economic Community of West Africa, ECOWAS

The fifteen nations of Economic Community of West Africa, ECOWAS, with a population over 350 million, have been seeking to find a way to improve the regional economy of all the nations in the region. Eight of those countries are Francophone nations within the CFA Franc system, another seven have their own currencies and central bank systems. As a region, two-thirds of the economic product and 60% of the population is Nigerian. For this purpose, there has been extensive negotiations between the 15 nations over a 20-year period to create a unified currency, which has been named the ECO. The ECO was supposed to have gone into effect in 2020 but the necessary agreements to do so have run into great difficulty. The full story of all the twists and turns in this, is not for this book, however the following observations should be made.

As is being currently proposed, the adoption of a unified currency for ECOWAS nations would be worse than the current situation. That is because the sovereignty required for national directed development and financing of needed projects would be even less than what it is now.

First, the monetary union that has been in the making for 20 years is modelled on the European Union creation of the Euro. Many of the criteria that nations would have to meet and comply with are like the criteria European nations must meet. Second, the monetary union proposal is being guided by the West African Monetary Institute which is closely linked to the European Monetary Institute that designed the Euro. According to their web site *"The West African Monetary Institute (WAMI/Institute) was set up in Accra, Ghana, in January 2001 and began operations in March 2001. The Institute is to undertake technical preparations for the establishment of a common West African Central Bank and the launching of a single currency for the West African Monetary Zone."* With the Euro being the worst disaster economically for the nations of Europe, how could its copy do any good for West Africa?

The attempts to escape the ills of the current situation, will only be made worse by a monetary union of this type. Most importantly, this is because the individual nations would have surrendered all their economic sovereignty to a West African Central Bank that will emit currency and set conditions without any nation in the region having any say. Even worse, the elected officials of all these 15 African nations, and all the regional leaders would have to submit to the dictates of monetarist technocrats administering the single currency and central bank, exactly the problem that is destroying a much more developed Europe.

SECOND LAW PART V: THE FAILURE OF BOTH LIBERAL AND MARXIST ECONOMICS IN AFRICA

One must ask why there is such a problem in realizing, or even understanding the concept of a modern sovereign credit system whose conceptual basis is fully developed in the three reports that U.S. Treasury Secretary Alexander Hamilton's submitted to the first U.S. Congress in 1792. Understanding why this is the case will have the greatest liberating effect on the ideological mental shackles of the false debate between Liberal and Marxist economics.

THE TWO GREAT MISSIONERS OF CIVILIZATION.

The British empire never debates its true philosophical enemies. Rather the empire tries to control the debate between two faulty ideologies, while their true philosophical enemy is obscured, never mentioned, and never taught in universities. Four or five generations later there is no one with a memory of what was really the issue. During the cold war, Africans were caught between these two false ideologies, one based on Adam Smith and his continuation up to and including Keynes and the Austrian free market schools, and the other based on Karl Marx and his continuation in the Communist and Socialist parties, the Soviet Union, and Maoist China. It is important to note that the British created Marxist ideology, and Marxist materialism as a false counter to Adam Smith and the liberal school in order to help obfuscate and prevent the adoption of the ideas of Alexander Hamilton and his successors by opponents of the British empire.

The classical liberal ideology on economics is based on greed as the driver of economic development and is pure evil. It is the nation, not greed, that organizes and drives the economic development on behalf of a vision of the future rooted in the general welfare of the community. The Marxist ideology, on the other hand, gets confused around the concept of the proletariat and class conscience. That somehow the overthrow of the capitalist class will lead to a dictatorship of the proletariat that will somehow usher in economic justice through the redistribution of the wealth. Neither ideology understands physical economics. For one, the working class never overthrew any so-called capitalist society in history. All the modern socialist and communist revolutions were primarily either peasant revolts against oppressive landlords and feudalist economic structures, or national liberation wars. The first such successful revolution in the 20th century was not the 1917 Bolshevik revolution, rather it was the 1910 Mexican Revolution.

The origin of the concept of the modern nation state was not in capitalism as Marx and others claim in their dialectical materialist ideology. The modern concept of the nation emerged out of the European Renaissance with Renaissance philosophers such as Nicolas of Cusa, and the scientific work of Brunelleschi, and later with Leonardo da Vinci, and the creator of the modern citizen militia, Machiavelli. The modern nation state, otherwise called the "commonwealth" has always promoted the economic development of the nation against the forces of feudalism, and financial powers such as the Venetian bankers. The very concept of a nation goes against both capitalist free market and Marxist ideology.

Today China, after much suffering, has adopted the earlier pre-Marxist economics of Hamilton, Mathew Carey, Henry Carey, and Friedrich List embodied in List's work, The National System of Political Economy. Marx never promoted economic development policies, only revolution. This system of nationalist economics was known in the 19th Century as the "American System," its enemy was known as the "British System," the system of economics that today dominates the world.

In the Marxist view, the issue of creating a revolution lies in developing "class consciousness" within a population to carry out the "class struggle" that overthrows the unjust yoke, in the case of Africa, of neo-colonialism. To do this the Marxist revolutionary must recruit cadre from a small number of middle-class intellectuals, or military cadre, dedicated to organizing the seizure of state power on behalf of a "proletariat" that does not yet exist. The dilemma in this is how does one psychologically transform a tribal, rural, agrarian, less educated population into the army of the revolution against neo-colonial overlords?

Some of the methods for doing this are explored by Martinique psychologist, Franz Fanon. These methods can be described as "purgative" violence against the "oppressor," in which the act of violence causes and is the individual liberation from oppression. That the chains of submission to the oppressor are broken in the violent act. This approach to creating revolutionary armies through the practice of purgative violence coheres in part with the Marxist idea of "class struggle." It is alleged that Julius Neyrere in Tanzania was involved in training future leaders of Africa in this method. Among those that are alleged to have been influenced by Neyrere in this are Yoweri Museveni of Uganda, Paul Kegame of Rwanda, and Laurent Kabila of the Democratic Republic of the Congo, and others. The problem with this approach is that anyone can use it, such as foreign financed mercenaries, jihadis, warlords, and insurgents of all kinds.

The Hamiltonian, or earlier American System approach to defeating neo-colonialism is based on the idea of economic progress. It is the development of manufacturers and infrastructure that changes lives, and the effect of economic progress on the self-conception of individuals is the most revolutionary influence. In economics the conceptual issue in obtaining for the nation the power of sovereign credit is not based on class conflict, but rather it based on what Henry Carey termed, "the harmony of interest." The farmer, the manufacturer, the worker, the whole society has an interest in the development of the nation. In a nation that has sovereignty and can finance thereby its own economic development, there is no inherent class conflict. The problem as such has never been the haves versus the have nots. Redistributing the wealth after any revolution does not change the level of poverty. Only the development of the physical economy can increase the living standards of the people.

The impediment to improving the lives of a people has been the existence of a continuous empire, with a memory going back to Venice around 1000 A.D. This continuous empire with its collective memory still runs most of our world. It is an empire that has moved from Venice, to Amsterdam, to London. It is a centrally coordinated intelligence empire, a divide and conquer empire of permanent wars like the Crusades, or the 150 years of religious wars in Europe from 1492 to 1648, or the current irregular wars overrunning the Middle East, and Africa, and threatening Central Asia. It is an integrated financial empire. Since the early 1600's it is the anti-Renaissance philosophical empire of the Enlightenment, or today, Liberalism. It is also a cultural empire promoting the corruption of the individual against any loyalty to the community or the nation. It can promote class warfare and run both sides of it. It is the enemy of sovereignty. This enemy can only be defeated by a concert of nations. The opportunity to do this is occurring currently, which is why understanding this is so important. This is what Marxism does not acknowledge.

Erie Canal at Salina Street, Syracuse, N.Y., 1904

This was the principal issue in the U.S. Civil War between the agrarian Jeffersonian, Southern slavocracy, and the Hamiltonian effort to industrialize that took hold in the North. It was a race between two systems in for control of the Americas. The U.S. agrarian slave system was part of the integrated global system of cheap labor that strangled the planet. It opposed the development of manufactures, and infrastructure, and was fanatically opposed to economic progress. The economic event that decided the future defeat of the slave system of America was the building of the Eire canal, completed in 1825, that connected the Port of New York with the Great Lakes and the mid-West of the U.S. Without the Eire canal, the North was economically pinned to the Atlantic Coast. This is a key lesson for all Africans; this is how to defeat neo-colonialism. The current propaganda war against China began in earnest when China announced the Belt and Road initiative and began to move towards extending it to Africa. The infrastructure development plans for the economic integration of Africa is the greatest strategic threat to the neo-colonial financial system. The claim is that China will not be able to deal with all the problems of corruption, etc., or China is just another imperialist power doing the same.

China's general view is that if you develop Africa, a productive and connected working-class identity will emerge that will be the new glue to unify internally nations with otherwise neo-colonial manipulated divisions. This is Alexander Hamilton with Chinese characteristics. It is the economic development that unifies and transforms a tribal identity into a national identity without doing any harm to the tribal identity. This effort by China is being accused of being a new oppressive empire in the making. What is not discussed is, who benefits from this? The people of both China and Africa benefit. Who benefits from the European neo-colonial model? Not the people of Europe, nor the people of Africa, but the plundering imperial oligarchy. This is also part of LaRouche's Second Law.

SECOND LAW PART VI: THE CHINESE APPROACH, THE BELT AND ROAD, AND ITS PROBLEMS IN AFRICA

China's adoption of Belt and Road Initiative and its extension into Africa was a daring move. It was done as the alternative to the internationally financed permanent irregular wars that have been unleashed on the planet by the imperial forces who wished to fully conquer the world after the collapse of the Soviet Union. This irregular war financed by the offshore financial system, much of it drug money, in the hundreds of billions of dollars per year, with private armies and U.S. interventionism, could only be successful in a world where there is no hope in the future, where desperate poverty rules. Russia's intervention in Syria to begin to resist this would have not been as successful without the future economic potential benefits of the Belt and Road. This was a civilizational intervention. Poverty is the greatest force for the corruption of nations and the actions that bring the hope of eliminating poverty is the greatest force that can be deployed against corruption, and these kinds of permanent wars.

THE WORLD LAND BRIDGE

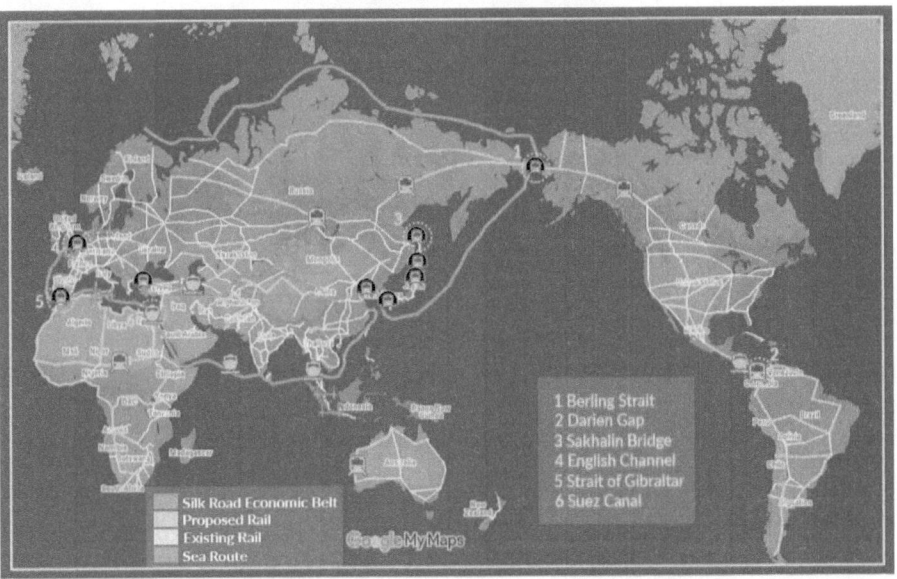

A screenshot of the World Landbridge Interactive Map from
www.Larouchepac.com

China's effort to build infrastructure in Africa on a large scale, which is only beginning, poses many difficulties. First, there is no true sovereign credit system in any Africa nation. As well, all African nations are already saddled with debts they cannot pay. All these debts need to be cancelled outright since the African nations have paid those debts many times over. To invest in Africa to build the infrastructure, China must go around this with their own financing credit system which is of a different type than the credit of the international banking system.

Nairobi Terminus ('Madaraka Express') is a railway station on the Mombasa–Nairobi Standard Gauge Railway at Nairobi, Kenya.
Photo by: Macabe5387

If an African country had a sovereign credit system, China could propose what was proposed by Iraq recently which was stopped. That a portion of the proceeds of raw material and commodity exports from a country be placed in a national sovereign development financial facility of that nation. This development financial facility would function essentially as a national bank and could lend ten times that portion in direct loans to African development. The use of these loans locally increases the commercial activity and savings of the population.

As the infrastructure grows, such as rail and decent roads, the cost of transport goes way down, and the potential for local investments along the transportation corridors goes way up, capturing much of the savings that would otherwise go into the offshore financial jurisdiction of the City of London. Whenever an African nation threatens these kinds of sovereign actions, their leaders are attacked, called corrupt, and the international funds begin flowing to the opposition, or to irregular warfare operations. Libya is the extreme case in this sense. What happened to Thomas Sankara in Burkina Faso is another example. All African leaders who were making genuine headway in the direction of developing their nations have either been overthrown or forced to bend to the international system.

In this situation China is using Chinese policy banks to create the credit. Chinese financial agreements are based on the intentions agreed to in the Memorandum of Understanding, or MOU's that is signed prior to any credit issued. These agreements are based on the future physical wealth creation that is expected from the investments in the infrastructure projects. This is different from loans of the international London based financial system. The London financial system uses the IMF's "structural adjustment" agreements as the guarantor of future repayment of debt. Thus, instead of an MOU centered on future physical wealth creation, the loans from the London based system are premised on reducing the sovereignty of the African nation through the direct interference in national sovereignty that the IMF's structural agreements cause.

Once an agreement of this type is made, it is easy for the system of financial speculation to manipulate the international market price of the both products being produced by African nations, as well as necessary products being imported. The unanticipated consequences of a loss of revenue based on the international market reduces the means to pay debts, and leads to a process of increasing indebtedness and a further increasing need to borrow, ending in more "structural adjustments" and an increasing loss of sovereignty.

In the Chinese system, the financing of projects is in principle different. For one, the Chinese concept of an agreement is different than that of the Western international rules-based order concept of an agreement. The Western idea of an agreement is that the agreement is the letter of the law, a la Shakespeare's Merchant of Venice. If the contract says a "pound of flesh" one must live up to the contract otherwise there is no law. In the Chinese concept, the issue is not the contract, but the "relationship." The contract is invalid if the effects of the contract are not mutually beneficial. If the contract isn't working, it can be changed by mutual agreement. Two current examples of this are the Grand Ethiopian Renaissance Dam in Ethiopia, where China reorganized the 10-year loan into a 30-year loan. The other is in Sri Lanka where the debt for building the port was also reorganized without punitive measures. In other cases, China has been willing to forgive some of the debt.

The Western media mouthpieces of Liberal Neo-Colonialism shriek at China's "lack of transparency" and "opaque, non-disclosure of its agreements" with African nations. That is because the agreement is a relationship and subject to change based on the circumstances. The issue is not

the payment of the debt, BUT WHAT THE DEBT CREATES. If the debt is not creating wealth greater than the cost of the debt, then ultimately, the debt cannot be paid. If a debt is knowingly being contracted that cannot be paid, it is considered by Confucian Chinese culture to be wrongly intended and in principle illegitimate, regardless of what the contract says. The import of this is that in principle, all the neo-colonial powers have been criminals in their economic dealings with Africa. That is because they have wanted debt slavery for wealth transfer, but not debt for development. The debt and interest keep growing while the means to pay keep shrinking. So, when those in the West complains about corruption in Africa, they need only to look at themselves and the criminal model they have imposed on Africa.

Currently Africa is carrying over $500 billion in foreign debt, of which a little over $100 billion is held by China. Except for Chinese investment in infrastructure, little if any of Africa's debt burden was designed to create future physical wealth. This emphatically calls into question the legitimacy of most of Africa's foreign debt. Any future debt contracted by African nations must be governed by the intent to contribute to the full industrialization of Africa. Such an intent guarantees the value of the debt in the future wealth that industrialization creates.

The claim that China is merely using the Belt and Road to gain influence for Chinese hegemony is false. Quite the opposite, if Africa fully industrializes with its young population, it will leap ahead of China and the rest of the world. If so, why would China support the development of Africa, if China were seeking hegemony? Rather, China is operating from the standpoint of the future physical economy of the planet: China has no future, nor does the planet have a future, if Africa is not developed.

Regardless of all the problems in seeking to develop Africa, for China, the development of Africa is a civilizational imperative. Unfortunately, China cannot develop Africa on her own and by herself. That is because first, China by herself cannot pay for the all the projects needed that together would raise Africa to a new platform. Second, China is operating in a system of global finance which is designed to prevent development. Third, it was China's intention to use the development of Africa as a way of helping to expand the involvement of the U.S. and European nations as partners in what is called, "win-win," to the benefit of not just China and Africa, but to the benefit as well of the industrialized West. This has not materialized as much as had been hoped, due to sanctions, threats, financial warfare directed at those who would participate, and an increasing anti-China propaganda war climate.

Nevertheless, China has made major inroads in laying some of the foundations for the infrastructure transformation of Africa.

Russia has also joined the process by promising to make nuclear power available to African nations. Then there are those who say that China does not have the intention to link all of Africa by high-speed standard gauge rail. That Chinese intentions are imperial only, and even if China is well meaning, everyone knows that it is impossible to develop such a "corrupt and disunited place." Those saying this will do everything they can to stymie the linking of all Africa by rail. But the development of Africa is a planet wide priority of extreme necessity, regardless of the current opposition and subterfuge by Western elites against the development of Africa. This is also part of LaRouche's Second Law.

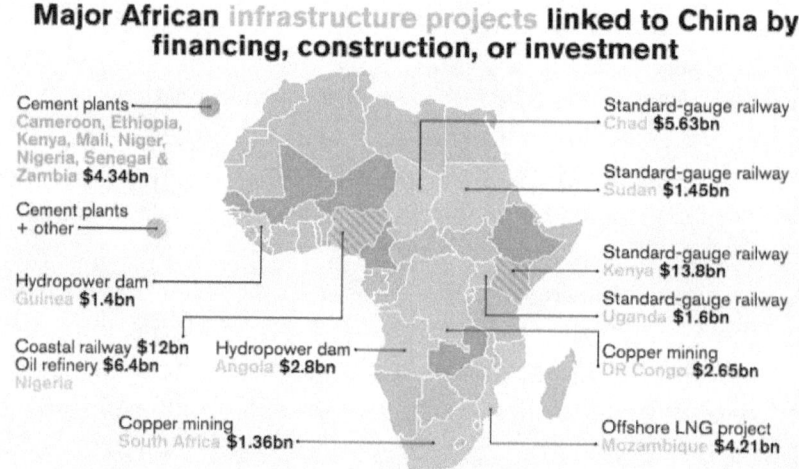

Major African infrastructure projects **linked to China by financing, construction, or investment**

Cement plants —
Cameroon, Ethiopia, Kenya, Mali, Niger, Nigeria, Senegal & Zambia **$4.34bn**

Cement plants + other —

Hydropower dam —
Guinea **$1.4bn**

Coastal railway **$12bn**
Oil refinery **$6.4bn**
Nigeria

Copper mining
South Africa **$1.36bn** —

Hydropower dam —
Angola **$2.8bn**

Standard-gauge railway
Chad **$5.63bn**

Standard-gauge railway
Sudan **$1.45bn**

Standard-gauge railway
Kenya **$13.8bn**

Standard-gauge railway
Uganda **$1.6bn**

Copper mining
DR Congo **$2.65bn**

Offshore LNG project
Mozambique **$4.21bn**

A screenshot of the Major African infrastructure projects linked to China, 2016. View complete pdf at: https://pubs.iied.org/G04095/

SECOND LAW PART VII: A CREDIT SYSTEM FOR AFRICAN NATIONS

By the time this is being read, the entire global financial system will either have collapsed, or is in the process of collapse. The COVID-19 pandemic, the shutting down of the economic activity in response to the pandemic and the most likely effect on the world economy and its financial system will end the "rules-based system" which was already in the process of ending. No nation that wishes to survive will be willing to continue following the "rules-based system" of the City of London and its neo-colonial arrangements. African nations will be on their own. They will have to end all payment on their external debt just to survive. Without the health infrastructure to deal with the COVID-19 situation, a significant part of the African population could be in jeopardy of dying, either of famine caused by the financial crisis or the pandemic.

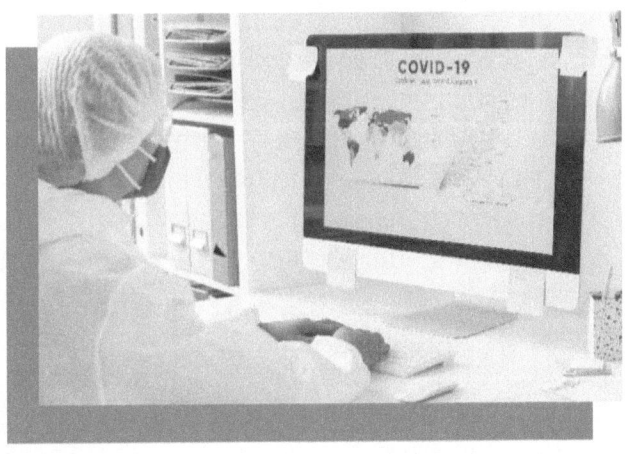

If there is any time when it is opportune for an African nation to move in and create a sovereign credit system, this would be the time, the time when the neo-colonial, globalized "just in time" supply chain breaks down. Above all else, African nations must revive their domestic agriculture to feed their people. In this respect a sovereign domestic credit system in each African nation would be a good starting point

Our first modern example of how a sovereign domestic credit system can work is contained in the memorandum of understanding signed in September 2019 between China and Iraq. A portion of the oil revenue of Iraq is placed in a sovereign lending financial facility overseen by the Iraqi government. This facility then makes loans in the ten-fold range of the oil revenue seed capital.

These loans are dedicated for reconstructing Iraqi infrastructure in partnership with Chinese construction firms and backed by China in the form of insurance on the loans. In this situation the Iraqi government does not go into debt, but instead is able to use a portion of the oil revenue in a leveraged way. These loans then circulate as credit internally in Iraq. This kind of arrangement is what Lyndon LaRouche called oil-for-technology agreements. Unfortunately, perhaps not coincidentally, immediately following the signing of the MOU between Iraq and China, protests and riots brought down the government of Prime Minister Mahdi of Iraq and the MOU is currently on hold.

Our second modern example is how Egypt recently built the expansion of the Suez Canal. The government issued a large, small denomination bond to the Egyptian citizenry, enough to pay for the construction of the canal. The terms of the bond were attractive enough that subscription could be restricted to Egyptian citizens whose savings were used to purchase the bond. These bonds paid for the building of the canal in local currency, increased the circulation of capital for commercial activity in Egypt, and employed may Egyptians without going to the international financial markets for loans in billions of dollars, or billions of Euros.

Our third modern example is how Germany rebuilt its infrastructure and economy after WWII. In 1948 the Kreditanstalt fur Wieberaufbau (the institute for reconstruction KfW) was created with a capitalization of funds from the Marshall Plan. These funds became the basis of making loans to rebuild Germany, finance agriculture, and other key areas. The KfW was state owned and was modelled on the Reconstruction Finance Corporation of Franklin Roosevelt which financed the building up of the U.S. during the great depression and WWII. Sovereign credit institutions of this type are the actual ways economic development of the key infrastructure has occurred historically. International bankers are not interested in the welfare of any nation. African nations will ultimately have to establish sovereign national banks, or credit institutions of this type if African nations wish to escape poverty.

In the crisis of the collapse of the City of London global financial system, there is a battle between two different orientations for replacing the current Floating Exchange-Rate System. These two profoundly different orientations represent radically different outlooks on what the future of humanity should be. The outcome of which of these two orientations will emerge as the governing paradigm for the world will be determined politically. Only if African intellectuals and leaders have clarity on this, can Africans have some say in which of these orientations emerges.

Clerks of the Reconstruction of Finance and Commodity Credit Corporation checking and tabulating loans and interest on loan. Photo: www.loc.gov

One of these orientations involves the creation of a new international financial architecture centered on a fixed exchange system like what existed prior to 1971. This new international financial architecture will be called the New Bretton Woods System. It will emerge out of conferences between the major powers, China, Russia, India, the U.S., and perhaps some other nations, and will replace the current Floating Exchange-Rate System of speculation. An assessment will be made on the future physical economic development plans of each nation and from there each national currency will be fixed to a gold reserve standard and to all the other currencies. Gold will only be used as a mechanism of measurement to make future determinations if there is a need to change the fixed currency relationships between national currencies. No longer will there be an international reserve currency like the British Pound in the past, or the U.S. dollar, and Euro today. Nor will the Chinese Yuan or a basket of many currencies become the replacement for existing reserve currencies. This is what a fixed exchange system means. It means that nations do not have to maintain reserves of foreign currencies to protect themselves from speculative attacks on their domestic currency from the international financial vultures. For all nations this means a vast increase in available credit for economic development. Trade between nations can be done in local currencies without resorting to a reserve currency. This will be facilitated by the establishment of capital controls to stop capital flight, and currency clearing houses to assist in international trade. These measures will also end the offshore, financial secrecy jurisdictions, and give nations the sovereign capacity to collectively shut down the international drug trade, which is at the center of these secrecy jurisdictions.

In this system, international currency transactions will be for trade, and not for speculation, which currently is somewhere around 96% of currency transactions. Each nation will establish a sovereign credit system internally. Each nation will do this by replacing their central bank with a national bank and sovereign public financial institutions. The national bank will issue currency and/or monetize debt as credit through investment in major infrastructure projects that dramatically advance the physical economic productive power of the region in which a nation exists. The limit of such credit issue is the capacity of the economy and labor force to be engaged, and the credit issue can be expanded as that capacity grows. Under this global new financial architecture, the greatest increase in global wealth for the world will come from the industrialization and development of Africa's water, power, rail, and the development of the most important resource that exists on the planet, the minds and skills of the vast youth of Africa.

The issue over the establishment of a New Bretton Woods financial architecture is at the center of all strategic political warfare at the macro level since these ideas to do this were introduced to the world, beginning in 1975 with the proposed International Development Bank by Lyndon LaRouche. In the context of a collapse of the Floating Exchange-Rate System, it can be expected that Russia, China, and India, would be in favor of such a New Bretton Woods System. Other nations like Japan and the nations of Southeast Asia would probably also agree. It is precisely the likelihood that U.S. President Donald Trump might also support such a New Bretton Woods System that is the unspoken issue that is driving the attempt to derail or remove President Trump. Those forces that would prefer to go to nuclear war to prevent a New Bretton Woods, include the U.S. State Department, the U.S. Military Industrial Complex, the "deep state" U.S. intelligence agencies, the U.S. media, and most certainly the financial system of the City of London and Wall Street. All of these are part of the globally extended neo-colonial empire of the British with its intelligence agents, assets, and auxiliaries embedded in all nations, including China, and in all multi-lateral institutions.

The second orientation also has a system being proposed to replace the current collapsing Floating Exchange-Rate System. This is the system being proposed by the globally extended British Empire. This proposed system has been publicly presented by Mark Carney of the Bank of England. Those discussing this openly are Black Rock, the world's largest investment manager, the billionaire

Mike Bloomberg, and the climate change crowd. This involves giving the major central banks the power to decide the budgets of the relevant nations. It involves replacing the U.S. dollar as a reserve currency with a central bank generated and tightly controlled crypto currency. With such a crypto currency as the world's new reserve currency, the world's dollar denominated debt can be wiped out without the neo-colonial globally extended British empire losing control.

To make sure that nations do not take advantage of the collapse to promote economic development through whatever emerges from the collapse, investments in infrastructure will be prioritized to "sustainable" "green" projects that guarantee no development. This is the significance of the "Green New Deal." Those promoting this version of the replacement for the existing system, absolutely know, and intend, to use their new system to collapse the physical productive power of all nations, with the intended effect of collapsing the "relative potential population density" in order to cause mass death on the planet, and a culling of the human species, most specifically in Africa.

Failure or success under Trump, or with his replacement, in getting the U.S. to back such a plan is at the center of global political warfare. Most of the world, especially Russia and China will resist this. As a result, the attempt to implement this orientation, or any like it, will require the deployment of propaganda warfare, regime change, international terrorism, NATO, and the U.S. military. When U.S. Secretary of State Mike Pompeo and the U.S. and U.K. defense establishments say, "we are war with China," this is what they mean.

Many Africans have been calling into question China's intentions in Africa. One cannot properly understand China's real intentions without understanding the nature of the current conflict engulfing the world between these two opposed types of orientations. It is easy to say that China has only selfish interests. All British networks will say this, and are saying this, because China's Belt and Road Initiative, whether yet able to be built in Africa, is THEIR mortal enemy. Any African who gives credence to such an orientation being promoted by the British, wittingly, or not, is assisting in the planned implementation of mass genocide of the African population. If as an African, one thinks of getting a favored spot among the few who will not be killed, think again.

SECOND LAW PART VIII: A BRIEF SIDE NOTE ON THE ISSUE OF ILLICIT FINANCIAL FLOWS FROM AFRICA

Much has been made about illicit financial flows out of Africa being a key factor in the inability of Africa to develop. This is a factor, however, unfortunately, the entire debate around this can be used to obscure the bigger crime, the legal financial system that keeps Africa from developing. It is estimated by the Report of the High-Level Panel on Illicit Financial Flows from Africa Commissioned by the AU/ECA Conference of Ministers of Finance, Planning, and Economic Development that there is about $50 billion a year of illicit financial flows. But who talks about the legal financial flows out of Africa?

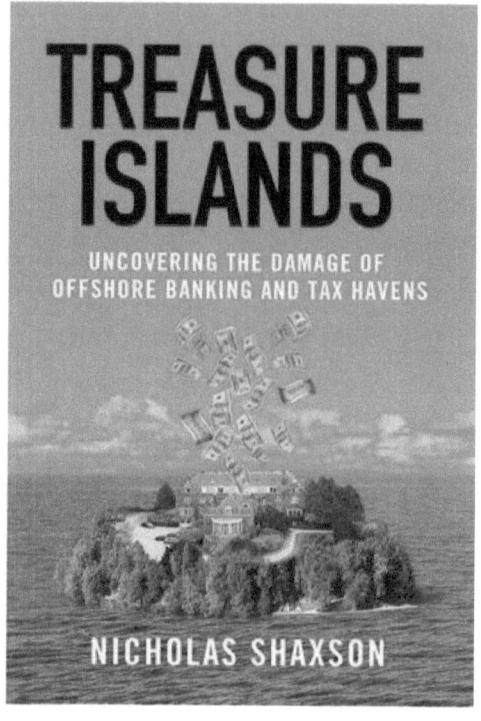

The entire international monetary system that Africa exists in, is a crime. The British who run Transparency International love to get everyone trying to chase the illicit part of the system, so nothing will be done about the legal bigger criminal part of the system which some estimates claim is the order of one trillion dollars that leaves Africa every year.

It is no accident that whenever African leaders try to do something for their people, Transparency International steps in to make accusations of corruption. The British empire corrupts you, and then uses that to hang you whenever they no longer need you. In a sovereign national credit system, within an international fixed exchange financial architecture, there are no offshore secrecy tax havens for drug money laundering banks that direct drug lords and mercenary armies all over the world. With current surveillance technology, and national military capabilities, the entire drug trade of the world could be wiped out in a few months. This is also a subsumed aspect of Lyndon LaRouche's Second Law.

What follows is the discussion of LaRouche's third law of Infrastructure as it pertains to Africa.

LAROUCHE'S FOUR LAWS

DISCUSSION OF THE THIRD LAW: INFRASTRUCTURE, HOW TO DEVELOP

THIRD LAW PART I: INFRASTRUCTURE IS THE TRUE NAME OF NATIONAL LIBERATION

The most spectacular statistic for the continental economy of Africa is that of trade. 90% of the trade of all African nations with all other nations is not with African nations. Only 10% of the trade of all African nations is between African nations. How is this possible? It is quite simple, "you can't go from here to there." From an economic standpoint, to be truthful, no African nations is really part of Africa. All African nations in economic terms are more part of Europe, part of the U.S., part of India, part of China, part of Saudi Arabia, part of Japan, part of Canada, part of Australia, part of everywhere but Africa. This is the physical description of neo-colonialism. Unless the transcontinental infrastructure is built that connects Africans to Africans, there is really no such thing, in integrated economic terms, as Africa.

What this means is that all the verbiage about African Unity, Pan Africanism, "we are all brothers," etc. will not work, unless there is a complete undying commitment to build the transportation corridors connecting African nations. These are the now proposed corridors that Chinese President Xi endorsed in 2014 with the African Union's vison 2063, which the plan for an African Integrated High-Speed Railway Network (AIHSRN) ratified by the African Union. The AIHSRN plan will connect 74 cities in six East-West and 4 North-South

corridors. The plan is fantastic, but implementing it is another issue, especially given the geopolitical and international financial opposition, the financial collapse, and the COVID-19 situation.

For those interested in the details of the plan these are the two links. The first one is 11 pages from the African Union on matters

involving the plan:
(https://au.int/web/sites/default/files/documents/32186-doc-towards_the_african_integrated_high_speed_railway_network_aihsrn_development-e.pdf)

The second is a 66-page detailed scoping study prepared for vison 2063 African Integrated High-Speed Railway Network Master Plan by a Canadian firm CPCS Transcom Limited for the African Union Commission (AUC) and the African Union Development Agency (AUDA) formerly NEPAD: *(http://www.nepadkenya.org/wp-content/uploads/2019/04/HSR-DSS-WP2-Project-Ranking-20190408-English.pdf)*

This scoping study goes through the parameters of potential traffic, economic return, political stability index, debt to GDP ratio of all the nations involved. What routes have the best chance of being built first. What pilot starter projects are currently feasible. The problem with the study is not the study as such, but rather the unforeseen factors that always change the scoping parameters.

Agenda 2063 is beautiful. The year 2063 will be the 100th anniversary of the founding of the Organization of African Unity. But what was done in the first seven years of the 50-year plan? The fundamental issue is the issue of political will and the drive to accomplish the objective. China can only do so much. Other nations must step up as well. We are already beginning to see in Nigeria, Kenya and other places that there is "not enough money", or there that there are environmental issues, or that the non-Chinese holders of African debt are putting pressures through multilateral institutions to force cut backs in investments in sections of the Vision 2063 plan. Who is kidding whom? Does anyone really think that the neo-colonial financial world will allow Vision 2063 to go through? The fulfilling of Vision 2063, which could be done on a crash basis in a few decades, or even less, is the end of the power of those currently running the world.

Only the development of infrastructure that trans-continentally connects Africa, can free Africa from its continued economic enslavement. This is a life and death issue for all Africans. This is the significance of understanding Lyndon LaRouche's Third Law on infrastructure.

THIRD LAW PART II: THE FIRST STEP, CONSTRUCTION BRIGADES, THE PRINCIPLE OF THE MONGE BRIGADES

All the money, all the credit, all the plans, all the good ideas mean nothing without the means to implement the building of infrastructure cheaply and quickly. Construction brigades under "army corps of engineers" type leadership is how it has been done in the past, and how on a continent-wide basis it will have to be done in Africa. China and other nations can help, but ALL African nations will have to organize their own military system of construction brigades, under most preferably, the leadership of military engineers. This is the greatest secret that the neo-colonialists do not want the leadership of African nations to initiate.

Gaspar Monge, a French mathematician, the inventor of descriptive geometry

The origin of this principle and method begins with a French military engineer, Gaspar Monge, during the period of the French Revolution when France was invaded by every power in Europe. Monge organized and trained young peasant boys in engineering and created a revolution in projective geometry that was used in construction and artillery. Not only did France thereby defeat its invaders, but these peasant lads who became engineers, demonstrated that from the feudal peasantry of France there could emerge the engineering means to build roads, canals, ports, fortresses, etc. This had never happened before, and the aristocracy of Europe was horrified, peasant lads becoming engineers? They are even more horrified today that something like this could happen to all of Africa.

But this revolution of peasant lads becoming engineers was not lost on other nations. In 1824 the military academy of the Army of the U.S. at West Point began a program based on the French example of creating engineers as the key part military training. This led to the creation of the U.S Army Corps of Engineers. It is the U.S. Army Corps of Engineers that built, or supervised the building of most of the key infrastructure that created the economic power of the United States. This is also what Franklin Roosevelt initiated in the 1930's in the U.S., with the CCC, or Civilian Conservation Corps. The unemployed youth were put to work in brigades doing construction and conservation, the results of which created the future disciplined workforce that transformed the U.S. economy during WWII.

After the Korean war, South Korea, the most underdeveloped part of Korea did the same thing. This is THE most essential lesson for Africa. It all begins with construction brigades. What South Korea did is induct a large number youth without skills into the military and put them to work in brigades building the initial infrastructure of South Korea. Over time these youth, from primarily rural backgrounds, developed the initial skills from which to eventually transition into manufacturing. All of this was paid for by local currency. South Korea is the only small undeveloped nation, outside of Singapore, that fully industrialized. Rejecting economic Liberalism combined with the military construction brigade principle was at the heart of South Korea's development.

In Africa, this would have to be done in a pan-African way. In the case of rail, each nation would have to initiate these construction brigades, preferably in a disciplined military form, to participate in building the rail infrastructure within their nation that connects with the transcontinental rail plan. One of the earlier African leaders who sought to mobilize the population into something like construction brigades was Thomas Sankara of Burkina Faso in his Committees for the Defense of the Revolution. There were problems with this, one of which was the isolation of Burkina Faso, and the lack of solidarity for this among neighboring African nations. But the concept of mobilizing the people to build the nation in brigades is valid. Today this can be done with the youth who desperately need employment and training and can be done on a pan-African basis. The advent of the internet and the revolution in communications through cell phones can help mobilize the youth of Africa to free Africa from neo-colonialism through construction brigades that will build the infrastructure of economic freedom.

"Pioneers of the Revolution", donning starred berets like Che Guevara. Photo by: Wikimedia

This construction process would be paid in local currencies, or in the case of how Egypt paid for the construction of the expansion of the Suez Canal. Giving African youth this mission of creating economic freedom through infrastructure building is the best way to combat the despair, and everyone for themselves kind of hopelessness that predominates. From this, a new African leadership of construction engineers can emerge, rather than street peddlers, thieves, beggars, and child soldiers.

Inducting tens of millions of young Africans into such brigade formations will be transformative, not just in the creation of infrastructure, but in the development of the discipline and the future skills of these youths. Perhaps even more important is that these youth of different ethnic and tribal areas would get to mix in a productive work setting from which would emerge a stronger national identity. True nation building begins in these construction brigades. No Chinese and European company, no matter how well intentioned can do this. Yes, China can train a lot of young people either in jobs overseen by the Chinese, or in academies, but only a nation can mobilize construction brigades of sufficient size that will provide the speed and momentum of construction needed to move African nations on the road to full industrialization.

Without these militarily conscripted patriotic youth construction brigades, paid for with local currency, Chinese technology and engineering can only build the infrastructure efficiently with primarily Chinese leadership cadre. Even if a large percentage of the work force employed by the Chinese is indigenous, this will not transfer the leadership skills, nor the spirit de corps required for future development projects. Because of this, China's best efforts to help Africa will always be criticized for not helping create within the nation being helped, the independent capacity to continue without the Chinese. Criticizing China for this is easy and is just another excuse for not having the leadership and courage to challenge the power of the neo-colonial masters with patriotic armies of engineering brigades of conscripted youth.

The mobilization of these construction brigades is the first major step in creating the internal economic demand for increased production of the construction materials that would be required for the various projects. Internally producing for the construction projects is the basis for expanding local industry and manufacturing. The water and energy for this manufacturing must come from

somewhere. This then creates a demand for increased electrical power, whether of hydropower, fossil fuels, or nuclear. This means the pan-African planners of the building of the necessary infrastructure must also plan on where the water and power for increased manufacturing must come from. With this comes a need for understanding the idea of a bill of materials for all of this. The key is to make sure that fulfilling the bill of materials for these projects comes from as much as possible from either local manufacturing, or the manufacturing of neighboring African nations. For this, a customs union among regional African nations may be needed to protect local manufacturing and the emerging inter African regional trade that these construction projects will begin to stimulate. Once the rail corridors are built, further use of customs unions would be helpful in further increasing the inter-African trade, which the corridors themselves will do. This approach was used by Friederich List in Germany starting in the 1850's to bring local areas of Germany together, which was the basis of the German nation and its industrial development.

But it all starts with the construction brigades. Without the construction brigades being fully mobilized in a coordinated pan-African way in accordance with a pan-African master plan for especially rail infrastructure, the first step to any African nation's industrialization will be missing. Without the military style training of a disciplined cadre of youth which begins in the construction brigades, African development will only be an idea, not a reality.

THIRD LAW PART III: STANDARD GAGE RAIL CORRIDORS, THE AFRICAN FARMER

The plan for an African Integrated High-Speed Railway Network (AIHSRN), approved in 2014 by the African Union (AU) consists of ten transcontinental rail corridors. Four of these are North-South, and six of these are East-West. All these rail corridors need to be high speed rail in the standard gage. There is no point of building anything of lesser capability than the current state of the art. What we want to deal with here is the fact that any feasibility study will tend to grossly underestimate the volume of traffic that such a rail corridor will have.

Artist concept of the proposed Rail Road Walkway Bikeway Pipeline and Electric Utility Bridge Over the Congo River between Brazzaville, Congo Republic and Kinshasa DRC Congo

The building of a rail transportation corridor is a revolutionary act. This is because every point along the corridor for a diameter of 100 kilometers is a point of development. In other words, things can be done. Otherwise nothing can be done. It is that simple. What can be done once a continental rail corridor has been built is dependent of the creative imagination of ordinary individuals, in this case mostly African farmers.

African farmers are the most important people in Africa, not just because they grow food. If their product cannot be transported somewhere why would they bother to grow those crops and vegetables, and staples for anything other than the most local markets? On the other hand, if there is rail from coast to coast, warehouses and brokers will appear, storage facilities will appear, towns and facilities connecting the farmer to more distant areas will appear, manufacturing servicing the new needs of the farmer will appear, new technology for increasing production will appear. Under these new conditions, the imagination of the African farmer is the key to the future. These ideas are also contained in Alexander Hamilton's report *On the Subject of Manufacturers,* ideas which have been suppressed for over a hundred years.

The problem is not primarily with the African farmer. The problem is isolation and lack of infrastructure connectivity, or you cannot go from here to there. The advent of cell phones is great, but that even makes it more imperative to have the infrastructure in order to realize the economic potential in the local area that exists with the employment of the youth of Africa. Otherwise, the cell phone connection to the outside world will only encourage migration of the most enterprising youth into the cities and beyond.

Workers load tobacco leaves on donkey cart, as no other transportation method can access the farm. Photo by: Big.H

It is this lack of connectivity that causes the cities to swell. Without connectivity the youth in many African nations do not see much opportunity and migrate to the cities, and sometimes to Europe or beyond. For instance, in Ghana the average age of a farmer is over 50 years. This lack of connectivity also leads to a huge drain of foreign exchange for food imports. This is caused by food insecurity that comes about because of the lack of food storage and distribution infrastructure, as well as lack of water management and electricity. The import of food, an attempt to compensate for these problems, only further discourages the development of local agriculture, a vicious cycle. No African nation can properly develop if it cannot solve the food problem. Solving the food problem can only occur in developing the infrastructure, or LaRouche's Third Law.

THIRD LAW PART IV: THE UNUSED MIRACLE OF THE CONGO RIVER, WATER AND ENERGY FOR AFRICA

The Congo river, its basin, and tributaries, involve ten nations in Africa centered around the Democratic Republic of the Congo (DRC). The lack of economic development in the area, especially the DRC, the poverty, with among the lowest per capita income, is the most incredible contrast to the potential of the miracle of the Congo river.

Aerial view of the Congo River near Kisangani, the capital of Orientale Province. Photo by: MONUSCO/Myriam Asmani

The amount of water that flows through the Congo and its tributaries is such that only a few percent of that flow diverted northward toward Lake Chad could transform Sub Sahara Africa in a project promoted by LaRouche back in 1979 called Transaqua. The Transaqua project has been recently revived by the nations around Lake Chad who are currently working with an Italian firm, Bonifica, and the Chinese on a feasibility study. The Transaqua project would end the droughts in the Sahel, revive Lake Chad, and provide the abundant water and hydropower needed for Central and West Africa.

The hydro power potential of the Congo River is in the order of 80 gigawatts, possibly more. This is enough electricity to power the entire continent. The Inga III dam near the mouth of the Congo, which is expected to generate initially 4.8 gigawatts, has been stalled in its construction for almost two decades. Without the hydroelectric potential of the Congo river, delivered by long distance transmission lines, Africa will have a difficult time industrializing. This electricity is required to expand transportation corridors, electrify rural areas, cities, as well as areas of manufacturing. Most importantly, having this kind of abundant electricity will greatly increase the productivity of the African farmer.

Obtaining the financing for getting these key dams built on the Congo river is not possible in the current global monetary system. The issue according to the Western financial experts is demand. The claim is that there is no demand. How is that possible when there is a whole continent with over a billion people in need of this electricity?

The African Union has made building the Inga III dam and harnessing the power of the Congo River a key part of its vision 2063. Since the vision 2063 was announced in 2013, South Africa has pledged the

The Inga dams barrage, on the lower Congo River near Matadi. Photo by: Alaindg

purchase of 2.5 gigawatts of power to get the incentive for the financing and the construction going. Since then both the governments of South Africa and the Democratic Republic of the Congo have been under attack from environmental NGO's who claim that the necessary transmission lines are environmentally hazardous to the population of the DRC. The other source of attack is from the budget cutters saying that the transmission lines are too expensive, and South Africa can get the same amount of electricity from two huge coal plants that are projected to be built. That the entire project is a waste of funds for South Africa. These attacks are motivated by Western neo-colonial forces. Deliberately missing in these attacks is the fact that Inga III and subsequent hydro projects to be built on the Congo River is part of the 2063 OAU vision for the industrialization of all of Africa. Without the increased power from the Congo River it will be difficult to have the power throughout Africa to develop the 10 transcontinental rail corridors, and everything else. This is another example of the subterfuge of neo-colonialism and their use of the international money system to prevent the necessary development of Africa.

In a sovereign credit system, nations create the credit and build these dams. Demand is not an issue. Demand will always come after these projects are built. That is because the building of the dam triggers the massive latent demand that exists for the consumption of the hydropower just because the dam has been built. The situation with Inga III parallels the story of the construction of the immense Grand Coulee dam in the U.S. The regional power company, the local political elite, and the financiers of Wall Street were totally opposed to the Grand Coulee dam being built. The reasons given were that there was no demand for the electricity, it was not profitable to the investors, and it was a waste of money. This was during the 1930's Great Depression in the U.S. It took the mobilization of a local newspaper editor and the general public to finally get the U.S. government to build the dam. The building of such dams and the rural electrification program of FDR in the 1930's was a key factor in the dramatic increase of the output of the American farmer.

Building the Inga III and many other necessary dams is a political issue and has nothing to do with demand. Not building these hydropower projects along the Congo River is another vicious cycle preventing the development of Africa. Harnessing the hydropower of the Congo River is another key part of LaRouche's Third Law applied to Africa. Without LaRouche's Third Law being implemented in terms of rail corridors, energy and water infrastructure, **pan-Africanism is pan-slavery.**

LAROUCHE'S FOUR LAWS

DISCUSSION OF THE FOURTH LAW: AFRICA NEEDS A FUSION AND SPACE PROGRAM

FOURTH LAW PART I: FUSION ENERGY AND THE SPACE PROGRAM ARE VITAL TO THE DEVELOPMENT OF AFRICA AND VICE-VERSA

The future platform for humanity which will result in the biggest economic revolution in human history is attainment of the fusion energy economic platform. The energy flux density of fusion is so great that any cubic mile of rock anywhere on the surface of the planet can, through a plasma torch process, be ionized and the elements therein separated with magnetic fields into resources for use in manufacturing.

All areas of the economic activity of humanity will be revolutionized. Some of those revolutions in materials processing are the creation of new isotopes, and the formation of many new unique composites and alloys for new inventions and industries not yet conceived. The fusion energy economic platform will also bring numerous revolutions in medicine as the electromagnetic properties of living systems become better known and used to cure diseases.

Within the fusion energy economic platform space travel becomes economically and abundantly feasible. All manner of space vehicles driven by fusion ion propulsion systems will be able to have constant acceleration and deceleration making a trip to Mars within a week possible. Through constant acceleration and deceleration gravitational fields can be created for the human cargo on board the space vehicle.

In the Fusion energy platform, the resource base shifts from materials to the ability of young geniuses to make scientific discoveries. In this manner within a fusion based economic platform the human species finally becomes autotropic, meaning no longer dependent on the sun and its products for existence. In this sense this fusion revolution is as significant in human history as the original discovery of fire.

However, from a geopolitical standpoint the prospect of a knowledge based full fusion based economic revolution is the greatest nightmare for the racist, imperial neo-colonial elite and oligarchy. This potential is well understood and feared and is the basis of why the green climate emergency mobilization is being done to castrate the economic potential of the planet to make it to the fusion energy platform. This is to be done by shutting down the massive increase of fossil fuels needed to expand the world economy sufficiently to be able reach the fusion economic platform.

This is where Africa is a central player in whether humanity can reach the fusion energy economic platform. This is where understanding LaRouche's economic ideas is key. To get to a  fusion energy economic platform the division of physically productive labor must increase by an order of magnitude. While the world's population has been increasing; except for China, the percentage of operatives involved in the physical productive part of the world economy has been decreasing. Larger and larger portions of the population have been shifted into non-productive employment. Much of that non-productive employment is in the swollen cities of the impoverished parts of the world of individuals just trying to survive in the informal economy. Some of the non-productive employment is in the entertainment, tourist, and sports industries. Then there are the functionaries, the bureaucracies, the armies, and the service economy of the more developed nations, this includes servicing the masters of the financial system whose financial activity and profit is the very essence of non-productive activity.

To get to a fusion based global economy, a reindustrialization of the more developed parts of the world is essential. However, most importantly, the full industrialization of Africa is the indispensable key for humanity to have the increased division of productive labor to be able to reach the fusion platform. Without the productive transformation of Africa, it is unlikely that humanity will reach the fusion platform. This is understood by the City of London system and its racist neo-colonial elite. This is why Lyndon LaRouche and his legacy is demonized and attacked in all Western media, and why most who agree with his ideas are fearful to admit so in public.

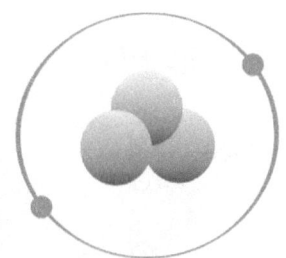

Helium 3 (^{3}He) consist of 2, protons and 1 neutron

The most efficient fuel for the future production on fusion is Helium 3. Helium 3 only exists in abundance on the surface of the moon. China, Russia, India, and the U.S. under Trump are committed, if allowed, to vector their space programs to the objective of establishing on the moon the industrial capacity to obtain this Helium 3. In this manner the development of fusion energy and the space program are interlinked.

African nations need to begin establishing their own space research and fusion research programs in order to develop Africa's future in space and fusion. On the one hand the industrial development of Africa is indispensable to the global effort to reach the fusion energy platform and space age. On the other hand, Africa must also participate in the scientific renaissance to develop the advance scientific capabilities of the necessary reality of the fusion and space travel age. This part of LaRouche's science of physical economics and the Fourth Law.

FOURTH LAW PART II: THE SCIENCE DRIVER AND MACHINE TOOL PRINCIPLE

In LaRouche's science of physical economics, future economic wealth does not come from increasing the exploitation of existing resources, or from decreasing the cost of labor as is commonly believed. These common beliefs lead to shortages of resources and an increasing inefficiency of the power of labor. Future wealth always lies in the undiscovered scientific principles that transform the productive potential of an economy. All efforts to conserve apparent finite resources by decreasing economic activity is the greatest threat to the existence of the human species. This effort to conserve lowers the future potential for realizing the expanded economic potential of scientific breakthroughs. Trying to decrease the cost of labor by decreasing the living standards only lowers the potential for having the quality of labor and skilled workforce required to assimilate scientific breakthroughs.

In this respect since the 1970's, since the ending of the Bretton Woods system, humanity, from a physical productive potential standpoint, has been going backwards. Only China, and some parts of Asia have been going against the tide of the monetarist destructive grip over the world economy of the modern neo-colonialism of the post-1971 system.

This is the science driver principle. Discoveries in science, nurtured by a nation, within a future oriented society, with an increasingly advanced skilled workforce is what drives an economy and the increase of future productive potential. The way the science driver principle works is through two interconnected sub-principles connected to the science driver principle. One of these is called the principle of technological spinoffs. The other is called the machine tool principle. The science driver principle and the two sub-principles work best under conditions of a crash program such as the Manhattan Project, or the Apollo Moon program.

In the Apollo moon program, because it was a crash program, many scientific disciplines came together not just to do experiments, but to actually build working prototypes which required solving key problems in production, inventing whole new apparatuses to make entirely new materials, and most of all constructing the new machine tools required for creating the prototypes. Every area of science is involved. From this came innumerable scientific spinoffs that have defined the beginning of our space age. However, the future promising process of further space exploration, and further technological spinoffs after landing on the moon was stopped for political reasons, and today it is principally China which is picking up where the Apollo program would have otherwise headed.

In the process of inventing and creating new apparatuses, new machine tools are also created. These new machine tools become the basis for revolutions in the productive apparatus of the economy as small and medium size entrepreneurs discover new and novel uses for the new machine tools. This is a key part of understanding LaRouche's science of physical economics and the Fourth Law.

FOURTH LAW PART III: CREATING THE FUTURE IDENTITY OF YOUTH

In LaRouche's Fourth Law, the future defines the present. In the racist neo-colonial system, the present is defined by the past. It is the youth in the period of childhood and adolescence that develop the dreams and ideas of what they wish to become which lays the foundation for the future of a nation.

The primary intention of modern neo-colonialism is to crush these dreams with rock-music, drugs, degenerate culture, strange sexual concerns, and enforcing a primary focus on sensual gratification. Africans for the most part have been resisting these efforts at the destruction of the youth by trying to preserve family values and traditional cultures. This is very understandable. This, however, is not enough. The youth of Africa must be given a dream. This is also what China is trying to do with its youth. However, for decades China's one child policy, which China now realizes was a mistake, has limited the number of youths for this dream. This is not the case for Africa.

The dream that Africa must give to its youth is the dream of fusion power and a space program and the future that that represents. Without such dreams shared by all African nations together with their youth, the past will always determine the present. This is also part of LaRouche's Fourth Law.

CONCLUSION: A SHARED VISION

It is claimed by Archaeologists and physical Anthropologists that the modern form of human beings originated and emerged out of Africa. That genetically all humans on the planet are descendants of Africa. If, indeed, Africa is the birthplace of modern humanity, then it is now Africa's turn to be the birthplace of the ultimate global end to neo-colonial economic slavery.

This must be the shared vision of all Africans, whether living in Africa, or living outside of Africa. This vision must be used to also organize non-Africans to the reality of their fate if Africa is not developed. The non-African must come to understand that only in assisting Africa to achieve this vison of economic liberation, can the rest of humanity repay its ancestral debt. Repaying that ancestral debt is also key to the future survival, as well, of all non-Africans.

Africa will and must become the economic super giant of the future, greater than America, Europe, China, or India. In doing so, humanity will be blessed by the youth and vigorous vitality of an emerging Africa, indispensably necessary for lifting from its current condition of despair, wars, disease, and famine, all of humanity.

Africa, you have the youth. You have the numbers. Go forward! Use the physical economic science of Lyndon LaRouche.

ABOUT THE AUTHORS

THOMAS P. FULLER

Mr. Fuller is an advocate for the Family unit as a driver of national economic policy. Founder of Ximura Consulting LLC, Mr. Fuller is a well-respected Indigenous American leader of Amen ascent. He is also an Ethnoecologist, activist, public speaker, educator, as well as entrepreneur.

Mr. Fuller is a sponsor and co-author of a trilogy of detailed technical, economic and environmental analysis of infrastructure development needs in Sub Saharan Africa. This trilogy includes the Civilian Conservation Corps (CCC) proposal for sub-Sahara Africa.

Mr. Fuller has spent over 35 years of research and analysis in developing ways to counter the European and U.S. immoral plundering of the indigenous people of Africa, the Americas, and the world, and seeks to create a world which is not subservient to the U.S. and European methods of state sanctioned assassinations, counterintelligence manipulations, and genocide used to enforce the poverty of indigenous peoples.

ABOUT THE AUTHORS

PAUL GLUMAZ

Mr. Glumaz studied at Columbia University in the late 1960's and 1970's in the areas of Cultural and Economic Anthropology. Mr. Glumaz has been active in spreading the ideas and policies of Lyndon LaRouche for the last 46 years.

He is noted for three articles:

1) Lewis Henry Morgan and the Racist Roots of Anthropology
   https://21sci-tech.com/Subscriptions/Archive/2004_Sp.pdf
2) The Hideous Revolution in Science, which is about the revolution of Darwin and Huxley.
   https://larouchepub.com/eiw/public/2015/eirv42n24-20150612/18-29_4224.pdf
3) Then and Now: British Imperial Policy Means Famine.
   https://larouchepub.com/other/2008/3517brit_imperial_famine.html